# *NOT NICE*

## by

# LINDA LANTERMAN

The characters in this book are fictional with the exception of some California elected women included to frame the narrative. These public figures are portrayed in fictional actions and circumstances. All other characters and events in this book are products of the author's imagination and should not be construed as real.

ISBN: 0-7596-3164-6 (e-book)
ISBN: 0-7596-3165-4 (Paperback)
ISBN: 1-4033-1803-4 (Rocket Book)

This book is printed on acid free paper.

Second Edition

1stBooks – rev. 03/20/03

*For my parents*

*Eunice Vivian and Walter H. Coupe*

*And in Memory of*
*Margaret*

Special thanks to Livvy Coupe, Melanie Caster, Wallis Leslie, for their assistance and to Bev Barnett, Ann Elliott and Dee Demorest and who encouraged and inspired me. Thanks to my husband, Doug, and to John, Margaret, Jeff and Angela for their patience and love. I owe a huge debt of thanks to Kate Karpilow and the past, present and future members of California Elected Women for Education and Research, at California State University, Sacramento. My thanks to Jan Provan, the Sierra Writers and to my original Bay Area writers' group: Jo Ann Daugherty, Vicky Mlyniec, Sandy Saidak, and Anatole Wilson who read my earliest draft. Thanks also to Mary Rosseau, Mary Wallace, Jane Stefani, Jan Edwards, Judy Mutch, Marilyn Shodiss, Carol Crowley and Diane Whitman.

Special thanks, also, to Bev Lane, the Town of Danville and to the community of the Fremont Union High School District, which covers the cities of Cupertino and Sunnyvale and parts of Saratoga, Santa Clara, San Jose, and Los Altos.

To all those who are active in any political campaign for public education, I salute you. Most especially, I thank Margaret Abe, Barbara and Ed Irvin, Thelma Atkins, Ruth Fitch, Mickey and Dick Wheat, Christopher Wall, David Stone, Donda and Jack Crittenden, Barbara and Fred Guard, Barbara Mardesich, Sharon and Michael Ward, Joann and Tom Tanabe, Dr. Betty Pacheco, Nancy Tivol, Ed Frank, Paul and Lupe Rutter, Terry Bibbens, Tina and Shlomo Bustnay, Nancy and Ron Calhoun, David and Marion Cleaver, Pat and Joe Digiovanni, Solveig and Norm Fjeldheim, Marzette Goforth, Elaine Yen, Linda Gregory, Dr. Colleen Wilcox, Joe Hamilton, Mike Hawkes, Phyllis Graham, Don and Ann Hines, The Honorable Nancy Hoffman, Beth McDaniel, Tim McDaniel, Kathryn and T.N. Ho, Peter and Gloria Hom, Mary and Leonardo Martin, Charity Webb, Dee and Denis Imazeki, Jim and Pat Jackson, Lall and Shabnam Jain, Nick Ferentino, Fran Grinels, Lolita Foster, Louise Renne, Ethel and Dieter Kopal, Rosemary and Pete Tuana, Bob and Barbara Koppel, Delia Ybarra, Karen Lilly, Margaret and Hsing Kung, Roy and Penny Lave, Pat Castillo, Janice Matsumura, Jim and

Shirley McCabe, Dianne and Regis McKenna, Becky and Jim Morgan, Ralph Mann, Mike Raffetto, Mary Lou Lyon, Roger Halstead, Shannon McKay, Louise and Carl Merino, Dr. Damon Nalty, Dr. Bob Wilson, Steve Nakano, Ann and Bud Oliver, Barbara and Burt Olsen, Alice and Tobru Ota, Roberta Pabst, Vauna Pipal, John Plungy, Deborah Weinberg, Dorothy Emerson, Natalie and Norm Pond, Bud and Charlotte Rix, Lila Rogers, Art and Kathy Ryan, Janine Stark, Dr. Paul Sakamoto, Elaine Ho, Judy Snook, Alice Farnham, Libby Spector, Agnes Correa, Congresswoman Anna Eshoo, Lorraine and Carol Steele, Mary Stone, Michael and Beth Szymanski, Anne and Jim Wall, Laura Kidwiler, Marilyn and Dave Wasmuth, Eleanor and Masao Watanabe, Ruth and Bill Foster, Gene Longinetti, Helga and Bill Waterfield, Carol Welter, The Honorable Jean Wetenkamp, Scott Wetenkamp, Marybeth Smith, Joan and Ellery Williams, Miho and Kio Yamane, Carla and Kent Zilliox, Forrest Williams, Marie San Antonio, Kathy Sportello, Helen Mineta, the Michael Miller family, Jim Walsh, and so many others.

# *NOT NICE*

# Chapter 1

## January 1992

Carol Steadhold pushed the throttle harder. Her fingers clutched and unclutched the wheel, lacquered nails flickering. "His thesis was that everyone has her dark side," she said. "Some expert! Some psychology of campaigning workshop! No one challenged him. The discussion floated way too long. Silly."

Highway signs, like flash cards, announced exits for the city of Davis on their right. Her friend, Diane Lind, watched the university and the surrounding flat farmland, green only so long as the winter rains would keep it that way. Carol began weaving through slower cars. Without moving her head, Diane glanced from the moderate traffic, to the speed indicator bouncing between seventy-seven and eighty-three, but said nothing. The president of California Elected Women was speeding.

"You made a better choice with the Legislative Analyst's update on education instead of the psycho-babble I sat through," Carol said. "The distinguished professor made it sound like everyone is evil. We're all barely able to hold ourselves in check. The more controlled we are, the worse we are."

"Carol, we've all done things we wish we hadn't. Made mistakes. We begin to learn from our mistakes as infants," said Diane.

1

"He made it sound like we were capable of stealing from each other, killing each other! Come on. Could you kill someone, Diane? — Could you?"

Diane laughed. "Well, I've certainly wished death on a few people, from time to time." She made a point of looking at the speedometer.

Carol turned to watch her friend, her eyes off the road for a long moment. Diane looked forward for her and said, "You should know better than to ask a fellow politician such a question. Oops, careful. Car — "

Carol slowed slightly. "Don't make light of it. Give me a straight answer."

Diane folded her arms. "People don't know how they will react under extreme conditions. Wars, disasters, plagues, famines — it's obscene to be cavalier about discussing good and evil in such circumstances. Words lose their meaning."

"It's a matter of will, values. Being strong, that's all," Carol said.

Diane was going to go into her mini-lesson mode, about the basic goodness of people and how it's the little things more than the big ones that bait ethical traps, but Carol took her foot off the gas.

A motorcycle cop pulled up beside them in the middle lane and pointed at Carol. With exaggerated deliberation, he signaled for her to slow down. She did, and he sped on. "Now there's a really good person," Carol said.

Diane grinned, adjusted her glasses and asked, "You sure you don't have government plates on this car?"

Carol sighed. "Guess I'm getting worked up over nothing. Roger and I are going down to Pebble Beach next weekend. It's Canby International business, but it'll be a weekend away for us, a chance to relax, I hope."

\* \* \*

2

Carol licked moisture from her lips and hoped the sun had hit the tennis courts first. A blanket of fog, dissipating unevenly, bounced the surf sounds inland through the trees and carried the smell of salt spray. On the curving path through the ancient Monterey pines, Shade Nettle, Canby International's VP of Finance, fell in step with Carol and began questioning her about her husband's home computer. Shade struggled to keep pace, his shirt buttons straining to contain his paunch. Carol slowed, then continued her trot. Shade had lots of questions, pushy questions. How many hours did Roger spend working at home? What special projects was he working on? "Slow down a minute, Carol. Please."

"I'm not home every night of the week, Shade. It's budget development time. Check with Roger."

"I've tried, but you know how it is. He's a VP. I'm a VP. We're always too busy."

Shade flicked his cigarette into the pine needles along the side of the path. Carol leaped on it, grinding it in circles with her tennis shoe. "Are you crazy?" she asked. "I hate people who do that."

"Sorry. Grass is still wet. No need to overreact.

"Has Roger mentioned anything unusual about work?"

Ignoring Shade as much as possible, Carol picked up the butt and carried it to the receptacle further down the path.

"In his telephone conversations, then. I assume you talk by phone?" The man didn't seem to realize his rudeness. Carol shook her head. "Shade, I've got a tennis match. Go away!"

Carol Steadhold had managed to keep the time open to join her husband for the weekend. Evert Johns, Canby International's president, appealed to her to attend, and she had rearranged her schedule. It meant a weekend with Roger on the Monterey peninsula. Upon reflection, she realized it was a working weekend for Roger, and she had forgotten what a boor Shade could be. Canby International was hosting a Japanese customer. Contract negotiations were nearly complete, which meant nothing was settled and time was running out. That much she

3

understood, but she was surprised not to have had more information about her role.

Roger said, "Just be the charming, nice lady you are. Evert wants to let my being married to an important government official speak for itself." Carol laughed. They both knew being the mayor of a small town like Danville was not that important.

"You're president of California Elected Women. Anyway, it's strictly social, hon."

Carol waved the thought away. "Strictly social," she said. "Okay, but nothing is more political than a meeting you have to describe as 'strictly social.' For all the criticism directed at government, even the greenest member of the town staff gives better briefings than I've had about this weekend."

Carol lost her match to one of the Japanese vice presidents' wives who turned out to be Midori Sato, world ranked when she was a junior player. Playing her best tennis in years, Carol went down three and two, and knew she was lucky to get the two games in the last set.

When she returned to her room, she found the maid cleaning the bathroom. "Did your husband find his computer?"

"My husband's on the golf course, since nine this morning."

The maid went white. "Oh! He didn't take anything! I watched him. He said he couldn't find his computer and wondered if he left it here. I thought he was — " She glanced at her list. "He said he was Mr. Steadhold."

"What'd he look like?" asked Carol. The maid's description was vague. Carol called the desk and asked that the staff be advised. Her jewelry was safe. Neither Roger nor she had packed a laptop.

"I don't think it's industrial espionage," Roger said, when she told him. He alerted the Canby people and the Japanese contingent.

At dinner, Carol found herself within conversational range of Shade and Angie Nettle. Angie smiled and nodded automatically while her husband discussed the merits of German and Japanese beers with Mr. Sato. Carol rolled her eyes at the extended conversation, and Midori raised a delicate hand to her face, hiding her smile.

From beer, Shade went into monologues on hotel security, finance, software and then weapons. He asked Mr. Sato about Samurai swords, permitted the man four sentences, then said, "I know exactly what you mean. I collect antique rifles."

"Ah, from a special historical period, Mr. Nettle?" The Satos gave no indication of their dinner partner's breach of etiquette.

"The Napoleonic era."

Shade continued talking, Carol noticed, until his roast beef was placed in front of him. Later, Shade suspended eating to interrupt Roger and Carol's conversation with their Japanese counterparts. He cleared his throat and said, "Carol, what do you think about the governor's proposal to consolidate the different bay area jurisdictions into one and reduce the cost of government? Sounds good to me. Cut the bureaucracy. Save the taxpayers' money."

"Did you ask me that question because you want to know what I think, or merely as a pretext to expound your own views?" Carol asked. Shade gave a choking cough.

"Hear. Hear," said Evert Johns, seated at the end of the table.

"Shade, you're brilliant in finance, but best to leave the politics to others."

Carol reddened at her lapse of self-control. She immediately apologized to Shade and began explaining the intricacies of the proposal and why it might not be the most cost-effective way to go. Shade, less enthusiastic than before, allowed others to join the discussion.

On their way back to their room, Carol said, "I shouldn't have cut Shade off like that. I spoke without thinking."

"Why?" Roger asked. "I wished I'd said it. Shade didn't mind. He shoots from the lip. Bluntness he understands. I think Ev was pleased to have our guests see Shade cut off by a woman."

Carol drew a breath as if to speak, but changed her mind. Roger unlocked their door. "Hope no one has been in our room this time."


Good fun and good food, the fund-raiser at the Jade Pavilion was Carol's second of the day, but she wasn't tired. When Chef Wang announced the main course, white-coated waiters strode into the room with covered platters held high, one for each table. Carol, the guest of honor, beamed as the heavy dish was placed in front of her and the lid removed, but it wasn't the fish she expected.

On a crisp, green bed of crumpled hundred dollar bills, with lichee nut eyes stuffed under puffy lids and red lips set in a toothy grimace, was the poached head of Shade Nettle. The diners applauded their appreciation while the waiters began serving.

Carol bolted upright in bed, gasping for breath and trying to calm her heart and twisting stomach. Roger awoke. "Honey?"

"Nightmare," Carol said. "Only a nightmare."

The next day, driving home from Pebble Beach through the rock formations near San Juan Bautista featured in the Hitchcock classic, <u>Vertigo</u>, Carol remembered her dream and described it to Roger. She also told him about all the questions Shade had asked her when she was going to play tennis.

"Strange, dear. Very strange," he said. "I know Shade's not your favorite person. Numbers guy, bit of a slob, but he tries. A mistake to bring him along this weekend, but we thought we needed him."

They were both quiet for a while. There was something about Shade, a sandpaper feeling. Carol didn't want to talk about him any more.

\* \* \*

Diane Lind always looked beyond the surface. Seeing the back side of things usually kept her out of trouble, an innate survival skill. She ran her fingers through her short, silver-streaked hair, fluffing the top, and checked off another name on her list. An elected school trustee, who also served on one of the governor's advisory committees, Diane knew she would be considered a traitor in the governor's office, but if the governor, or anyone else, did something she considered bad for kids, she would not keep still. She picked up the phone again and tapped in the number of Carol's direct line. She had consolidated her forces. It was time for the second part of her plan.

"Mayor Steadhold."

"Hello, Carol, It's Diane Lind."

"Yes, Diane."

"Thanks again for the ride to Sacramento last week. Today I'm calling about the governor's budget message. Have you looked at what it'll mean to Danville?"

"Not a very pleasant picture, if the legislature goes along. Cities will fight it."

"Schools will too. I hate to hand you a hot one, but some of my League of Cities friends and a couple of the county supervisors I've talked to are urging a coalition to head off the bloodbath. We don't need a free-for-all among the cities, counties, school districts, the university system and all the rest."

"No," said Carol, picking up a pencil.

Diane knew Carol probably felt prodded, but she felt Carol would not ignore a good idea merely for the sake of ego. Diane came to her main argument. "The divide and conquer strategy won't work, if we don't play. The organization is — "

"Which organization?"

"California Elected Women. We're positioned to take a leading role on this. We're non-partisan, have members at every level of government."

"I understand what you're saying, but the League of Cities hasn't issued anything on this yet," Carol said. "I'd like to see what they suggest."

"I've talked to Sunnyvale's mayor. She's past president of the League."

"Yes."

"She suggested having all the executive directors get together and talk. My thought is that you could set it up, a unity conference."

"Sounds like you've thought of everything, but I can't simply tell our executive director to do something like that on my own authority. Evelyn will tell me where to go. She will be polite, but she'll tell me all the same."

"As president of CEW, you could ask her to poll the board. Put the issue to them squarely. We have to try. Anything is better than fighting each other."

"Before you go too far with this, I should remind you there are a few goodies in the governor's proposal —."

"Only if we pull them away from each other. He's throwing a few handfuls of candy to the starving for the pleasure of watching us fight. Once we fight among ourselves, he'll say we aren't worthy and suggest we should be starved further."

"Always line up your ducks, do you, Diane?"

"Try to. Tell Evelyn where I stand. That'll be one less telephone call for her."

Conversations with Diane often went this way. Carol flicked her pencil back and forth, making tiny slash marks on the key word notes she'd taken. She stood and went to the expanse of glass looking out upon the town hall's young redwood trees, and studied her reflection. Her hair was going to gray, but not obviously so. It blended with her light coloring very nicely. The goldtone metal of her glasses framed blue eyes and gave her face a roundness it needed. Her features were delicate, well defined; a little sharp, she could hear her mother's voice mention again. She told herself she liked her professional appearance. She thought she looked like a mayor, only thinner. She turned back to her desk, resolved to add more color to her wardrobe, and called Sacramento.

8

CEW Director Evelyn Day came on the line, and Carol began at once. "On the governor's budget, I've been talking to a number of people throughout the Bay Area, and I think we need to put together a unity meeting...."

# Chapter 2

Canby International, Incorporated, built everything from dams to pipelines to nuclear power plants. The worldwide headquarters were in Oakland, California. The company was an engineering-construction corporation, which also could operate and manage a facility once they built it, if that was needed.

An open atmosphere, with low dividers and only occasional glass partitions, Canby International made it easy for the Director of Finance, Hsing Tom, to observe Shade Nettle without appearing to do so. Shade had summoned Hsing, but seemed unconcerned about making him wait. Nettle had become one of the company heroes, a decisive eccentric who seemed to guess right every time. Acquaintances knew Nettle was a Swiss citizen who liked imported beer and old guns. Few knew of his obsession with hacking.

Arriving as part of a tiny software firm Canby had acquired, Shade Nettle's skills quickly made him the number three man in the financial department. Shortly afterward, when both Canby's vice president and finance director retired, Nettle became Vice President of Finance. His job, while challenging, didn't have the exciting risk element of imminent disaster that being part of an organization of fifty-six employees had. He began to revamp his operation. Unassuming Hsing Tom, who had been with Canby for nineteen years, and a candidate for VP, become the director, Evert's choice, not Shade's.

Absently, Hsing touched the California Golden Bear in his lapel and lowered his eyes to the carpeting. Hsing's family had been in California for many years. His father had been a member of the Taiwan trade mission in San Francisco. Hsing attended Lowell High School and UC Berkeley. When his family returned to Taipei, Hsing stayed and became a U.S. citizen.

Hsing recognized Nettle's forcing him to wait twenty minutes was a power play, but he regarded it as the insecurity of the new vice president. He could hear Nettle's loud joking and pictured the man's close-cropped hair, watery, blood-shot eyes, and his beer gut jiggling with each laugh.

Finally, Nettle summoned him from the reception area. Hsing stepped into the office of the Vice President of Finance and Chief Financial Officer, and sat down stiffly in the armchair Nettle indicated. On the opposite wall were two Napoleonic rifles, in offset alignment, one above the other, pointing out the window. The office smelled of stale cigarette smoke and sweat, with a fake evergreen overlay.

"I understand your father is gravely ill, Hsing. I'm very sorry to hear that," the big man said.

Hsing thought it strange that Nettle had been so jolly on the phone only a few moments earlier. Nettle's serious expression now must be a mask. Genuine or not, it was an unwelcome intrusion into Hsing's personal pain.

"He has been diagnosed with acute leukemia, sir."

Hsing moved his eyes to the window and stared out into the feeble blue-gray of the winter sky. Nettle began again. "Taiwan is so far away. It must be very hard on you and the family. You're the only son, I believe?"

"Yes, the only child." More formal by nature than his immediate superior, Hsing glanced at the paper-strewn desk, the semi-hidden, unemptied ashtray, the askew tie and partially untucked shirt. These appearances belied the mind, Hsing reminded himself and braced for whatever it was Shade Nettle wanted to discuss.

"Hsing, I hope you will understand that I have your best interests at heart and certainly the best interest of Canby International when I say this." He paused, but Hsing, returning his eyes to the sky, said nothing.

"I've recommended your transfer to Taipei as our second in command of the operation there. It's quite an honor. Of course, it is a much smaller office than the headquarters here, but it's growing fast, and you will be invaluable to us there."

"Sir, my father has less than a month to live. I am leaving tomorrow to spend ten days with him — "

"I'm so deeply, deeply sorry, Hsing," Nettle shook his head and looked at the floor. "I understand. That's why I went ahead and made all the arrangements for you. Our executive officer there is beside himself with joy, absolutely. He can't believe we would part with you. When I first came to Canby, he told me you had the sharpest financial mind he had ever seen. Here, I have his fax. It's full of superlatives."

He shuffled through some papers, picked out the fax, dated a week earlier, and carried it around his desk to Hsing, whose mouth fell open in silent protest.

"Just take a look at that."

"How long? A temporary assignment? My family, my home — I don't understand."

"You remember the exec?"

"Of course, he was Director of Finance here before going to Taipei six years ago — "

"Good man, good man. I've met him just a couple of times, but I could tell right away. He's a good man."

Confusion and anger marked Hsing's usually placid features. His eyes tried to pierce the veil of words Shade Nettle waved like a skilled matador, waiting with his sword.

"You will have the same salary and benefits. Of course, that will be reevaluated in a year — in a matter of months, actually. You'll be able to settle your father's estate, comfort your mother, get things squared away. Evert hates to lose you. We all do, but I explained the situation, and he understands completely. He even feels it's an inspired move for the company. The exec has been asking for higher level support in that office for the past year. It's a terrible loss to the department, and to me but we'll have to tighten our belts and double up. We've been luckier than many companies that have to downsize in this economy, but a little belt tightening never hurt.

"Now I know this seems sudden, but I wanted to surprise you." Shade moved from his desk to stand over the Hsing's chair. He grabbed Hsing's hand in a pumping, relentless handshake while his left hand slipped to Hsing's shoulder and urged him up and out of his seat. The meeting was over.

Hsing rose but stopped and stiffened. "The internal audit is next month. We've been preparing for it. There are a number of new complications this year. Some very serious unresolved issues, those I reported to you last month, and the new irregularities we discussed."

"I've got it under control, Hsing. Don't worry. At a time like this you have to remember the most important thing is family. Evert mentioned that too."

The family part or the audit, Hsing wondered. His mind cleared. He had the picture now, and he didn't like it.

Nettle continued in his most congenial tone. "Convinced him we could go with an outside auditor checking random account codes to save time and money. That's the bottom line, isn't it? You know it is. Lots of good outfits capable of doing what we'll need done. We can get back to the full blown, Cadillac procedures when the economy improves."

Hsing's face was burning with shame, his heart thumping wildly at hearing his work trivialized, his life turned upside down. He was the last to know. They had omitted him from the game plan.

Hsing drew a deep breath. "My mother is dead. Five years ago. She died five years ago." Realizing that Nettle must think

13

him a fool, Hsing stood very straight, gave a slight bow of his head, turned and walked away.

He was going back to the accounting department when he heard a robust voice call out something about season tickets to the Cal basketball games. Hsing turned to see the lined but bright, smiling face of Roger Steadhold. Close friends since their days at Cal when they both played in the band, the two men faced an awkward pause.

Roger began again. "Please tell your father I pray for him and that my life has been enriched by the wonderful stories he told us each time he came to visit."

Hsing nodded. He realized that Roger didn't know about the transfer, but he was too ashamed to tell him.

Roger patted his friend's shoulder. "Have a safe trip, Hsing. Call when you get back. We'll get together for dinner at our place." Hsing nodded again, numbly, and kept going.

\* \* \*

Twelve weeks later Roger received an e-mail message from Hsing telling of his father's death and a bit about the new job in Taipei. The tone was somber and lacked the cheerfulness Hsing usually exhibited, even in adversity, except for one puzzling paragraph.

Remember the time the Straw Hatters were outdoing ourselves at the Cal-UCLA basketball game and we lost the melody? I have the old music from that game. Cannot understand where we messed up. Maybe you'll get a laugh from it. Take a look at it sometime for me. The current musicians might want to see it for the archives. By the way, my chief assistant, at headquarters, is a Cal Bear and a magician who never loses the melody.

14

Strange reference, Roger thought. The Straw Hat Band didn't use printed music at the basketball games, and Roger had no memory of any game where they'd lost the melody. He knew Hsing's chief assistant, a bone-thin woman who attended most meetings with Hsing and always had any of the needed backup. He made a mental note to talk to Shona Oliver.

The day after Roger received Hsing's message, Hsing's wife, May, telephoned. May would be teaching summer school at Oakland Technical High and had not accompanied her husband to Taipei. She asked if Roger could meet her during the lunch hour.

"My schedule's tight today. Will it take more than half an hour? You could come into the office or out to the house this evening."

"I only need five minutes, Roger. Mountain View Cemetery isn't far from Canby. You drive right up Piedmont Avenue. I'll be in my car in the administration building's main parking lot. I need to visit my mother's grave."

"I'll be there." Strange.

\*   \*   \*

It seemed to Roger the death business was booming. He had to park across the lot from May Tom. A light breeze rustled tall pines and eucalyptus. Dots of light doppled the pavement. Roger walked over to the car where Hsing's wife stood waiting by her open trunk and gave her a quick hug.

"I don't know what it is, Roger. Hsing left it for you. He telephoned and asked that I give it to you in private."

"Thanks. This whole box? What do you hear from him?"

"His father's death was difficult, but he's stoic about it, and he does feel he's making an important, positive difference in the Taipei office."

"The official word is he's revolutionized the office. The XO has recommended that Hsing be his replacement when he returns to the states next fall."

May didn't smile in acknowledgment of the compliment to her husband. She lowered her voice.

"Roger, Hsing is coming back here within the year, with or without Canby. Our families have been friends a long time. Please see what he has sent to you. I'll leave now."

The box was about the size of his shirt box from the laundry. A yellow three by three note stuck on top of some sheet music for "All Hail" stated "For Roger" and "Go Bears!" The box was about half full. Roger placed it in his trunk. He would go through it when he got home.

The manicured, old cemetery stretched up the hill and over the top. Roger drove up the winding road and stopped and walked among the graves a while. He breathed the eucalyptus scented air. The Oakland/Berkeley fire that destroyed so many homes had burned up to the cemetery's boundary, no further. Roger surveyed some of the blackened area from the cemetery's highest point, then drove back to work.

In his den that evening Roger found a stack of computer printouts under the sheet music. At least eight different account codes, in painfully small financial detail, filled the spreadsheets. Cal's motto "Let There Be Light," was written in Hsing's familiar lettering across the top of the first page. Roger began going through the data. He spent about twenty minutes thumbing through the printouts. He couldn't be sure that the data even pertained to Canby International. But it must. Three or four times in flipping through the pages, he came across a black ink notation in tiny but very neat writing "no documentation" or "cannot be verified." Hsing's senior accountant, Shona Oliver, had initialed each one. Social security numbers? Insurance claims?

Roger put it away carefully, making mental note to set aside some time to give this project the focus it was going to take. He already had two major proposals needing immediate review, on top of the usual crunch at the end of the fiscal year. And the annual stockholders' meeting preparation. Time was tight and he didn't know what he was after. Something was terribly wrong or

Hsing would not be asking for this kind of help, in this convoluted way.

# Chapter 3

## Spring 1992

The campaign season had begun, but only the strategists and the snipers at the front knew it. In the seven counties surrounding San Francisco Bay, Carol Steadhold and Diane Lind were picking up signals. Diane was a patient, relentless crusader who carefully studied the terrain and her adversaries. Carol dared to consider grasping an opportunity not easily granted to a woman. Both were selective idealists. One exercised power. One sought to understand it.

They came from different parties, but they had much in common. They were the same age and their children were grown. Both were hard hitters who enjoyed tennis and politics. They moved comfortably within their political systems, adept in tactics and effective enough to have made enemies. These two didn't know each other well enough to think about their differences.

Carol had served eight years on the council for the Town of Danville, an affluent, bedroom community, inland from the bay, in Contra Costa County. It was her second term as mayor.

On the Peninsula, Diane was a veteran trustee in a sprawling suburban high school district that blankets Sunnyvale and Cupertino and parts of four other cities in Santa Clara county,

California's Silicon Valley. The forty-two million dollar school district shoestring budget dwarfed the eight million town budget, but a mayor can dream of running for Congress. Others, too, were thinking of the congressional seat.

Carl Gard was trying out his usual line of banter on the yawning hostess at the Hidden Oak restaurant in Danville when Jack Smolders and a friend entered at one twenty-five p.m. The hostess straightened and pointed toward the private room, greeting Mr. Smolders by name. The men moved past brusquely, with no acknowledgment. A handsome, tall, lumbering man, Smolders had a slight limp, the result of repeated football trauma to his left knee. His stride, his thinning light brown hair and glasses aged him beyond his forty-two years.

His companion had square, rawboned features, and a similar athletic build, but much shorter. Carl knew Smolders only from the business pages and raised his eyebrows at the hostess in an exaggerated gesture that was supposed to communicate surprise. In fact, he seemed impressed, changing his line accordingly, while he ambled over to glance into the open doorway and then returned. The hostess picked up the phone to avoid talking to him. That simple ploy never stopped Carl, who continued his monologue in her general direction. His beautiful wife, Bea, finished in the restroom, and with a laugh, guided him toward the door, rescuing the hostess.

"Don't mind him. He's totally harmless."

"Well, I think we should stay, Dear. The big wigs are just arriving." Carl's baritone carried to the manager who walked quickly to the door of the private room and closed it. Carl, pleased with his part in the little drama, permitted himself to be led out.

At the History House reception that evening he came up behind the mayor. "Guess who I saw today."

"Oh, Carl. Good evening. It's always fun to see you. Where's Bea?"

"She's here somewhere, but I've got something to tell ya."

Carol eyed her friend thoughtfully. He nodded. She linked her arm in his and moved away from the gathering.

"Jack Smolders and his cronies had a meeting today. The hostess at the Hidden Oak even said his name."

"You're sure? Big man with limp?"

"I'm sure, I tell ya. Don't know who some of the others were, though."

"How about a short, stocky guy with blond hair and real pale blue eyes?"

"Yep, walked in with him."

"What about a tall, skinny man with bushy, gray eyebrows?"

"Maybe, maybe not. I only got a quick glance."

Carol ran through a number of physical descriptions. Carl confirmed that most had been present. He knew a couple of them and said, "When I saw those two together, I figured Danville was in for some major development you politicos at city hall haven't told us about."

"They're king-makers, Carl, outside the party organization, but the real power in Contra Costa County, on the Democratic side — both sides, sometimes. They usually meet very privately, in one of their own buildings away from eyes like yours. They must be casting about for a new congressional candidate."

"Fine. Now can we go somewhere and neck?"

"Oh hush, Carl. If someone ever takes you up on that, you'll have a heart attack. Thanks for the info, though."

Since she hadn't known about the meeting, she'd had no representative in the room. The omission stung her.

Carol's mind whirled with scenarios. The name Carol Steadhold must have come up at the Hidden Oak meeting, at least once. Someone might have said she was a nice lady, popular in Danville, unknown elsewhere. Others probably added that she should be cut down early, if she was thinking of the congressional race. She might pull the women's vote away from the judge. Damn!

After a nearly sleepless night, Carol startled Roger when she poured orange juice into his coffee cup at breakfast. She laughed with him about it, but moments later started pouring the milk for her puffed wheat into her juice glass. An earwig fell from the section of the Oakland Tribune she was reading and arched its pincers fiercely over its back. Carol thumped it with her heavy spoon, rolled it in her white paper napkin and crushed it again. Roger pushed back a wisp of wavy gray hair from his forehead, smiled and leveled his hazel eyes at his wife. He knew she was thinking about the restaurant meeting.

"They met without even telephoning. You sure they know you're interested?" he asked.

"I'm sure. I leak it to friends in Smolder's Walnut Creek office every chance I get. If I run, it'll be without that gang, at least in the beginning. They're ignoring me. It's going to be tough."

On his way out, he kissed her, forcing his way into her consciousness, if only momentarily. "Hi, honey. I'm here. If you make your move, I'm with you."

She murmured tenderly, and he was off to the Bay Area Rapid Transit station for the trip into Oakland. The news had shocked them. The incumbent congressman was serving his last two-year term; his struggle with prostate cancer had become public. November 1994 had seemed so distant, until news of the Hidden Oak meeting.

Carol called her friend and former campaign manager, and began without preamble, "Wallis, There's been a meeting."

"Yes —. Without you?"

"Right. At the Hidden Oak yesterday. Smolders and his group. You have any time this morning? To come over?"

"Sure. We should see who else is available. I'll try to reach a couple of people. You call a couple at your end of town. In an hour?"

"That's perfect. We'll set an evening meeting of the full group once we talk, even if only you and I can get together today."

Carol thought of the wider group of men and women among her close supporters who should be in on the early discussions. Her thoughts dashed ahead.

The party people will be no help at this stage, but she couldn't leave them out. Plug some of the party regulars into Wednesday afternoon. Make all the telephone calls to the big financial supporters by Thursday, if they can be reached during the end of June. Get started on the endorsement language by Friday. Nail down one or two important endorsements by the weekend. Damn! The Canby stockholders meeting. The thought jolted her. The meeting would shoot a whole afternoon. Although, she thought, she should leak her plans to Evert Johns. He always asked when she was going to run for Congress. It was just so premature. Work the room as the dutiful wife, get to everyone, but no mention of Congress — not without a grounded strategy, except privately to Evert. That's the way it will have to be. Save it for the company picnic in August. More appropriate then anyway.

Like snapshots, she visualized the August afternoon at Tilden Park: red, white and blue balloons, patriotic theme. Only one or two reporters alerted, friendly ones. Places for volunteers to sign up, invitations to a big bash fundraiser, all soft sell, no illegal arm-twisting. Her thoughts raced. Evert could take credit for asking her to run and trumpet the announcement to the whole company. She would make a good, short speech. Evert will say a few more words about what a great congresswoman she would be. Do the formal kick-off that night for the whole district. Powerful way to start.

*       *       *

Across the Bay, Diane Lind also was acutely aware of her upcoming campaign. In Cupertino, summer speakers for the weekly Rotary Club meeting were scarce. When the new county sheriff had to cancel, the vice president in charge of programs thought it would be a good time to invite the local school board presidents to discuss the state of the school districts. At Wednesday's meeting he strolled up to the superintendents of the elementary and high school districts who were engaged in conversation. "Good afternoon, ladies. I need a program for next week's meeting, and I thought we could address education."

"Great," they answered in unison.

"I thought it might be interesting to have your board presidents come in and each speak for, say, ten or twelve minutes."

The elementary district superintendent was visibly crestfallen. "I think our president might be going on vacation next week, but, of course, I'll check. If she can't be here, I'd be happy to fill in."

The superintendent of the high school district became serious. "Diane Lind would be very good," she said. "I'll call her this afternoon. If she can't make it, I volunteer to join my colleague here. Or, maybe you could schedule us sometime in the fall."

"Thank you, ladies. One program on our schools will be enough, in addition to having the students come in on occasion. Tell your board presidents they each can have fifteen minutes."

Diane wondered if Rotary had a rule against speakers who were running for reelection, but she snatched the opportunity in spite of having to share the podium with the elementary board president. If Rotary did have such a rule, was someone choosing to ignore it?

Several Rotarians had sent checks. Her campaign had begun before school was out. Publicly, things were quiet in the summer months, but privately, the real organization was taking hold. From her announcement letter, she had collected enough funds to print her brochure, and do her first mailing in the fall. She would be the first person to file, and she would be completely ready to go right after Labor Day when people would start to pay attention to the local races.

Diane walked into the spacious, main meeting room at Cupertino's new community center with its acoustics that bury voices in noise, to find many Rotarians had checked in early. She visited with a couple people she knew and thanked the program chairman for inviting her.

He said, "Diane, we have you sitting at the center table in front. May I escort you?"

"Only if you introduce me to those four gentlemen over there. I don't think I've met them."

"Of course, working the room, I see."

She had met three of the group before, but did not recall their names immediately. More importantly, the route to where the men were talking helped Diane avoid Agnes, a former board member and her confidant, Zel.

Another friend joined the little cluster of people around Diane and gave her a hug. "Diane, how nice to see you. I'm delighted that you're one of our speakers today."

The room filled rapidly. When Diane turned back toward her table, she was blocked. Zel, one of the two women she wanted to avoid, stood right in front of her. Zel was very close, smiling down from her three-inch height advantage. At five-seven, Diane got a good look at the woman's uneven, stained teeth.

"Diane! Hi. So, how did you manage to force your way onto the Rotary agenda in an election year?" Zel smiled expectantly, eyes bulging behind her oversized, sun-sensitive glasses, her palms twisted inward with all ten fingers aimed skyward, in front of Diane's face. "I mean, without equal time for the opposition?" She thrust her fingers toward the ceiling once more, face frozen and pitted, a gargoyle off her perch.

Diane refused to take even a half step backward.

"We're talking about education and the school district today. No one can file for election until August, so nothing's official. Am I going to have opposition?"

"I've heard some rumors. Oh, I've the greatest joke. Do you know why the Chinese eat so much rice?"

"Later, please." Diane turned to the Agnes, greeted her and said, "Beautiful ring." The expensively dressed Agnes, who had joined them, wore two heavy rings on one hand and three on the other. She glanced down at her hands as if wondering how to parry the remark.

"The fire opal. Actually, they're all lovely." Diane seemed instantly sorry she'd been catty.

"I was just asking Diane how she had the pull to get on the Rotary agenda," Zel reported to Agnes.

"Diane never hesitated to use her influence when I was on the board with her," said the woman with the jewelry.

Diane heard the words drip slowly from the woman's mouth and forgave herself for the ring remark. Her use of power was an old charge she'd heard from these two whenever she and they had been on different sides of an issue and Diane's argument carried the day.

"Real power comes when you give it away," Diane said. She had never convinced these two of this, but she tried again. "When you empower others."

She knew they thought the words were good. They had used the same words themselves. They simply didn't believe them. Diane tried to end it. "It's a political science thing."

Diane needed to move on, but she couldn't disentangle herself from more of the women's determined efforts to stop her. The superintendent of the high school district approached, cheerfully catching each of them in her great bear hug.

"Why, Agnes, Zel, I haven't seen you two for a while. Tell me what you have been doing."

With a quick pat of thanks to the superintendent and a wave, Diane was gone. Eleven tables of eight with a few open seats, she worked as much of the room as she could before being forced to sit and eat a few bites.

During the saccharine, informal introductions of the speakers, Diane glimpsed the ring woman's knowing look at her collaborator. Diane watched Agnes open her mouth slightly and slowly run her tongue over the sharp edges of her front teeth.

Having served with her for eight years, Diane recognized the habit. She wondered if Agnes cultivated the mannerism or if she were unaware of it. The woman did it this time right after the words, "such nice ladies," in the introduction. Diane was well aware that the 'nice lady' tag tended to undermine a strong leader who happened to be a woman.

The elementary district's board president spoke first, using twenty minutes of her allotted fifteen to gush about the wonders of each of the excellent elementary schools. From the table closest to the podium, Diane sat with calm, alert attention. Her superintendent made two obvious gestures of looking at her watch for the benefit of the program chairman, who failed to notice. The superintendent then bent her elbow, leaned her head in her palm and tapped her watch. Still the man failed to notice, but the speaker did. With a little laugh she promised to finish, and within an additional two minutes, actually did.

Diane left her notes in her chair, deciding to wing it. She used precious seconds to acknowledge the ring woman, another trustee in the audience, and her superintendent. She thanked the program chair for his introduction, but she began by taking exception to his words.

"While we do not want to be referred to as wicked women, 'nice ladies' doesn't do it. If he had used wicked women, the two guys who ducked out right after eating might still be here."

The group tittered, and she paused, smiling.

"There are one or two people in this room who know that I am not necessarily a nice lady. I bet they must have been quite startled by the reference."

Open laughter broke out from individual tables. One high school principal rose and saluted. Her superintendent smiled and nodded in agreement. Two close friends waved their hands in the air, then others who knew her less well. The ring woman rolled her eyes at her friend Zel and they smiled slyly and whispered to each other.

The nonsense was eating up too much time. Diane raised a hand for quiet and began.

"You've just heard many reasons to be proud of our elementary schools. An equal number of wonderful things can be said about our five high schools. The superintendents are members of this club and tell you constantly about our schools, sometimes more than you care to know. You sponsor many of our students and honor them at a special luncheon each year. You share our pride in their accomplishments and our distress in their failures, and when we fail them.

"So, today I'm going to present some ideas about where we must go in public education and why. I'm a tough sergeant in the fight for our kids, and I'm here for fresh recruits."

And she began. "We've all been a part of maintaining barriers to human potential, sometimes with the best of intentions, sometimes not. There are five points I'd planned to pursue today — "

"Good speech, Diane." The high school district superintendent walked to the parking lot with her. "I only hope you didn't bring up too many issues for people to absorb. You gave them so much to think about."

"What should I have omitted?"

"Everything you said is important. Maybe concentrate on one or two items and go more in depth, instead of five or six. The mood in the room became serious and reflective. Did you feel it?"

"I had just one crack at that group. I thought I was cutesy enough at the beginning. But you're probably right. I may have hit them too hard. They asked good questions at the end, though."

"Terrific questions. I'm going to have people talking to me for months about the issues you raised."

"That's what I want."

# Chapter 4

Before leaving for lunch, Director of Human Resources, Jake Hartig studied his image in the mirror he kept at eye level on his bookshelf. He ran two fingers over each eyebrow and then over his trim black mustache. He had expensive tastes in clothes. Good-looking, in his way, he was a slight, prim man, bald on top with a circle of black wavy hair from ear to ear. Twice divorced, he lived alone. For someone in his field, he was surprisingly ineffective with people, except that he read body language well. He liked the protection of hiding behind company rules, and he enjoyed reviewing personnel files, but he hated Canby International.

In the cafeteria, Jake asked for extra nuts on his Waldorf salad, no frosting on his square of carrot cake and an extra fork. He received them all with a smile, but when the cafeteria worker asked him a simple question about her changing her social security deduction, Jake glared at her. "See one of the clerks in benefits. That's why they're there. I have a lot on my mind today."

The employee hung her head, "Oh, sorry, Mr. Hartig. I — I — Never mind. I didn't mean to disturb you."

Jake would take a long lunch. He planned to work late tonight.

Since the board meeting only ran until ten p.m., Shade Nettle decided to head back upstairs with three giant peanut butter cookies, for an hour or two of private time on his computer. "What the hell —?" He dropped the cookies and charged into his office, hands clenched into fists. Jake was sitting at his computer. "You goddamned weasel! What the hell are you doing in my office?"

"Nothing better happen to me."

"What're you talking about? I'm going to tear your head off and shove it up your ass." Nettle grabbed across the desk but missed Jake, who stood pressed against the wall of glass overlooking the plaza.

"I've seen plenty, and I smell the stink of embezzlement."

"You're dead wrong. You've seen nothing. That baby's locked down tight. The only smell in here is you, you pissant slime. Trying to break into my computer... I'm reporting you first thing in the morning. After I tear your head off."

"Okay, Mr. Vice President, you do that, and I'll have to suggest an itemized review of certain account codes. I'll start small. Say workers' comp claims. See where that takes us before I throw in something bigger."

"Be my guest."

"How about your distinguished record in high school, the rumors about how you changed some grades on the permanent records, even charged some students to take the SAT for them."

"Nobody knows that. You bluffing son of a bitch. I'm Swiss, remember? You've got nothing. You can't prove shit. Get out of my office!"

"You came to this country when you were fifteen. About the high school stuff, I probably can't prove much, but it would be of compelling interest as part of an overall investigation. You could use my help."

"Get outta here."

Jake watched the larger man's eyes dart around the room. "I've got you by the balls, Shade. You need me."

"I work alone."

29

"Not any more. There are records I can bury or lose. I've got a few contacts in t —."

"This is entirely out of hand. You're a lunatic."

"Call me what you want, but my silence is golden, if you get my drift."

"Spare me. Sit down. Tell me what you think you've got."

Jake scurried from behind the desk to a seat at the far end of a small conference table. Shade Nettle took his usual posture, half-sitting on one end of the desk and watched the little jerk from Personnel. "So you think you have the upper hand against the VP of Finance, do you? Tell me what you've got."

"Me? I got nothing. I don't know a thing about any irregularities. Mr. Nettle is a brilliant financial officer who's always looking to save the company money, like on the new audit procedure."

Shade softened his tone. "You're a real bastard, Jake, in way over your head; but let's say maybe I could use some assistance. If you have something, why don't you turn me in? Why did you come nosing around anyway?"

"A hunch."

"If we're working together, you've gotta come clean."

"An offhand remark by one of the secretaries at lunch, Hsing's hurry-up transfer to Taipei. The new audit procedure, a bunch of little stuff no one else'll put together."

"I see." Shade ran his fingers down the length of his tie and back. He scratched at a soiled spot. "It's a quiet little operation, small enough not to raise suspicions. It only means twelve to fifteen thousand a year." You're really stupid, Jake, if you believe this. "We could up it to twenty, twenty-five without too much strain, since there are two of us. We'll split fifty-fifty, but I'm in charge and you take orders. No questions and complete secrecy."

"I'll need twenty thousand up front."

"You're talking two years' work for doing nothin'. Don't get greedy on me, Jake. You're involved now, the way the cops'll see it. Your bargaining power just diminished, and I've given this a hell of a lot more thought than you have. The banks have a bad habit of reporting unusual deposits. Don't louse up a good thing, pea brain."

"Okay, make it fifteen. And don't worry about the bank."

"Make it ten, and I can bring you the cash tomorrow. The year starts now. We distribute earnings every six months. Agreed?"

"Sure."

"There's some effort involved."

Jake seemed surprised.

"Yeah, Jake. You're not the only one who might be putting stuff together. Roger's been askin' a few questions."

"Steadhold?"

Shade ignored him. "Dumb questions. He doesn't suspect us. Doesn't even know what he's lookin' for." Nettle watched Jake get out his handkerchief and blot his perspiring forehead. "Time to ante up, Jake. You wanted in. Perhaps your contacts can find out where Roger's looking. He asked for some info from Accounting, nothin' important by itself, unless he's checkin' against something else we don't know about. We need to know what he has.

"How fast can you have someone snatch his briefcase? I think he's carrying whatever he has with him."

\* \* \*

"Hi, where were you at four fifteen?" Roger asked Shona, the chief accountant. "I thought we had a meeting."

"Sorry, Mr. Steadhold. Mind if I walk with you to your car instead? I don't want to get transferred to China if the wrong person sees me talking out of school."

"What's this all about?"

"Don't be upset, but something's wrong. I just wanted to let you know that I'll give you all the help I can. Last January, Hsing suspected something — someone, of stealing from the company. There were a number of odd, new account codes and procedures

31

instituted in the last six months to a year and no one seems to know where they came from. The records I was working on with Hsing disappeared when he left. I can generate only about a third of them from our computer files. Mr. Nettle told me not to worry and moved me off the audit. I think someone's messing with the system. I need this job. I don't know whom to trust. Hsing was your friend." Tears filled her eyes; a rivulet of mascara ran over her right cheekbone before she wiped it away with her fingers. They had stopped walking.

"There's a good Thai restaurant in Berkeley, on University, about half way up, going toward campus. I'll meet you there for lunch tomorrow at one. I'll have my secretary, Phyllis, call you with the name and address. She's a good person. She can say you're needed to cover a meeting for her in San Francisco, or something, if anyone wants to know."

"Good," she said. "I'll be there."

"By the way, Shona, I did receive an unusual package from Hsing."

# Chapter 5

Al Gonzales found a bench in the shade of an ancient oak on the fringes of the park that surrounds Lake Merritt. Drought or not, the park was too important to the people of Oakland to let the grass die or to run the risk of stressing the trees. The park received its necessary water allotment. Al was one of the city's citizens who enjoyed the green haven, the expanses of grass and water, the mature trees and the gardens. Carefully unwrapping his Casper's hot dog, he took time to appreciate the foot long creation with its fresh onion and tomato wedges, barely contained by the bun. He inhaled deeply. To Al, Casper's was another important Oakland institution.

A wiry, five foot five, Al's pleasant, open face and large, dark eyes reflected his giant optimism. In his freshly pressed, white shirt, the new twill slacks that he'd been saving, and polished shoes, he felt very confident. He had picked up his lunch and taken it with him downtown to be sure he wouldn't be late to his job interview a block away. He had half an hour to enjoy himself and some breath mints he hoped would cover the onion. The day was perfect, warm, but not too hot, and a cloudless sky of such a vibrant blue that he paused to absorb the color.

Across Grand Avenue's four lanes of busy traffic, Roger Steadhold strode down the sidewalk unaware that the street person he had passed two buildings back had turned and was following him. He did notice the hard look of a muscular man loitering at the newspaper racks who looked up and came toward him.

"Spare change, Mister?"

"Sorry, not today." Roger felt a twinge of guilt, but he was rushed. Without stopping, he switched his briefcase to his other hand.

"Aw, please, Mister. Business is bad. Canby dropped three points on the New York Exchange this morning." The man spread his arms wide, blocking Roger's path.

"What? Get out of my way!"

He hesitated and turned to escape, but the second man came up behind him. Suddenly the rough stucco of a building scraped his face, and he went down on one knee, more startled than hurt. He had been sandwiched and shoved against a wall. In less than four seconds, they had his briefcase.

"Hey — you goddamned thieves! Come back here!"

One assailant disappeared around the building, the other, with the briefcase, ran right into traffic and was attempting to get across Grand Avenue.

Happily chewing his first bite of lunch, Al noticed the commotion and saw the man, dodging cars, running to toward the park. Cars honked and screeched trying to avoid the thief and each other. To Al's amazement, the man angrily pounded the stolen briefcase on the hood of a car that had nearly knocked him down. Bellowing like a moose, the victim charged right into the street, looking neither way, just charging after the first guy like a Marine. Al put down his hot dog and moved to intercept the thief who was jumping the curb. He apparently didn't see Al in the shadows of the ancient oak.

Supervisor Marian Regal, driving an Alameda County car, was returning from a state transportation conference in Sacramento when she had to brake suddenly for a man running right through the traffic. She almost wished she had hit him when the man wheeled and bashed the hood of her car with a briefcase. The dent would be in the hood forever. Everyone would connect her with it, and she prided herself on taking good care of county property. She hit her horn, and the man ran on. She drove slowly looking for a place to pull over. In her rearview mirror, Marian could see someone tangling with the man who hit her car. As they rolled on the ground, a third man ran up and joined in. She punched in 911 and was talking to the police before she could find a place to stop at the curb.

She worked to control her anger with slow, deliberate speech.

"This is Marian Regal, Supervisorial District Two. I'm witnessing a crime in progress. My car has been assaulted by a thug who is now fighting with innocent bystanders trying to apprehend him. I'm near the intersection of Grand and Piedmont and need assistance at once."

"Ms. Regal, please confirm your location, the corner of Grand and Piedmont. Are you on Piedmont or Grand?" A woman's voice answered the call.

"I'm on Grand, heading toward Piedmont, going around the park, trying to find a parking place."

"What's the nature of the crime you witnessed?"

"Listen child, this man bolted right into moving traffic, right in front of my car. I nearly hit him, 'n I was in the middle lane. He got so upset, he bashed my car with his briefcase. That's the thanks I get for not leavin' him smeared all over the pavement."

"There's a fight going on now?"

"After the fool smashed my hood and yelled at me, he ran on over to the park, but someone tried to stop him, and then another man came running through the traffic, after him too. Last I looked, there was a big tussle goin' on. I can't see them now, too many cars."

Okay, Ms. Regal, we've got a unit in the area. Please stand by."

By the time Supervisor Regal slammed the car door and was marching back towards the men, a police siren wailed in the distance.

The two men had the thief subdued. Flat on the ground, his neck in a hammerlock, he saw a woman's high heels, then moved his eyes up to see Marian Regal. "Aw, shit."

The attractive African American supervisor had a reputation for zero tolerance for criminals. He had been forced to listen to one of her speeches when the police presence had been too evident to permit his usual working of the Memorial Day crowd, only one wallet that day, off a kid, with just four dollars and a library card in it.

The police officer assessed the scene. Roger, one of the two men who had subdued the suspect, started at once.

"This man stole my briefcase, officer."

"If you'll be patient, sir. I need to get Ms. Regal's statement first. She called in the emergency."

Marian Regal began before the officer had his notebook open. "I cannot believe the bad manners of some people. This idiot ran right through all that traffic. I nearly had to crash my car to avoid hittin' him, and he screams at me — me, the one who's just saved his pitiful life. Then he assaults the hood of my car, a county car, mind you, paid for by the citizens of Alameda County. He smashes that briefcase right down on it leavin' a big ol' dent for everyone to see.

"He's obviously the child of a broken home, not that being raised by a single mother, or a loving grandmother, needs to condemn anyone, but it's a strike in today's world. I've proposed the extension of playground hours and special programs for the youth of our city, but will those state politicians listen? No. Raise the money with more taxes and fees, they always say. After they scrape all those same taxes off the top for —."

"Can you tell me exactly what you saw, ma'am?"

"I told you. After he hit my car, he ran over here where this man stopped him and that man came right through the traffic after him. They were teaching him some manners for not stopping. If this contemptible excuse for a man had the opportunity for licensed pre-school when he was little, and all his immunizations and tutoring in the primary grades, an —."

Another patrol car arrived. "Here's another officer, ma'am. She'll take anything further you have to add." The female officer assessed the scene, alerted by the radio communications that a county supervisor was involved. The officer escorted the supervisor back to her car, and dutifully inspected the small dent in the hood.

Roger produced his identification and the key to his briefcase. The male officer handcuffed the suspect and began interviewing Roger and Al.

Al was missing his interview. He had a sore cheek and his shirt was ripped and grass-stained. His new slacks were wrinkled and grass-stained too. His good mood vanished. He appeared defeated and wondered out loud why he had become involved. "The worst of it is, I've missed my job interview for that cook's assistant job at The Golden Bear. I think I had a good shot at it. And look at that. The sea gulls got my lunch." He pointed to where two gulls were taking off from a bench with a foot long wiener between them while two others squawked and squabbled over the remains of the bun.

"I certainly appreciate what you did," Roger said. "That character might have gotten away if you hadn't stopped him. I'm Roger Steadhold, VP of Operations with Canby International. That briefcase is very important to me. Give me your name, address and phone number." Roger noted the information in a small, dark green notebook and then pulled out his wallet.

"We both could use some cleaning up. Take this for your lunch. I'll be in touch. It takes a special kind of person to do what you did. I appreciate it." He waved away Al's protest and stuffed a twenty into his shirt pocket.

Later that afternoon, Alice, Jake Hartig's secretary, was in his office reviewing the postings that needed to be filled. She rose to leave when the phone rang, but Hartig motioned her to stay. After a few words, he turned on the speakerphone so she could hear a vice president asking him for a favor.

"I understand, Roger, but there's a freeze on hiring. I mean if the guy was a whiz bang engineer, maybe. We've been invited to observe that project drilling for oil and gas in Sweden, and we don't have anyone free with that kind of expertise — hell, I don't think any company has a scientist that weird — but from what you told me, this Al Gonzales person is unskilled. Probably doesn't have a degree or anything. We aren't running a charity here."

"What about in the cafeteria, maintenance, or sweeping out the offices? He missed his interview at a restaurant when he caught the crook who was running off with my briefcase. He's a decent sort. I just think we could give him a break, that's all."

"Roger, we can interview him, but those jobs are filled with long term, good people. There's been no turnover for the last two years, and that's a record I'm proud of. You know how choosy we are about hiring. Why interview a guy just to wait-list him?"

At this point, Alice uncapped her neon pink highlighter and marked three positions on a sheet of job postings. She stood, placed the sheet on Jake's desk so he could not miss it, and left the office.

He glanced from the highlighted sheet to Alice's back headed out the door. "Bitch," said Jake, under his breath.

"What?" Roger asked.

"Not you — nothing."

"I want you to put him on, Jake. Find a place, any place, for the guy."

"No can do, Buddy."

Roger paused, then abruptly hung up. "No can do, huh? — Obviously we weren't too choosy when we hired you." What a bastard. The guy usually at least maintained a veneer of accommodation, Roger thought. He picked up the phone again and called home. His wife's voice clicked onto the line and invited him to leave a message. Carol's voice, even recorded, had a soothing effect. He probably had sworn more times today than in the past ten years. No point in it.

"Hi, Carol. I've had a pretty exciting day. Don't hire a new gardener, I may have one for us. Hope this isn't a council meeting night." Then he remembered it wasn't Wednesday so he added, "See you around six thirty, Honey. Bye."

What would a cook know about gardening? Well, he could offer.

Roger went past the glass partition to where his secretary, Phyllis, was lacing her tennis shoes. "After lunch would you see if someone could run this jacket down the street to the tailor's and get it sewn up?" he asked her. "The shoulder seams gave way."

She laughed. "Looks like it will need to go to the cleaners after that. I'll take it myself. A couple of us are going to be going that way on our walk."

Roger emptied his pockets onto his desk and handed her the jacket. "Watch out for muggers!"

"They better watch out for us." She called from the outer office. "Nobody messes with me."

Roger ran his hand over the raw skin on his face. Phyllis was probably right, he thought and smiled to himself. I just had military training. She raised three sons to try out for professional football.

He freshened up as best he could and left his office to see if he could still get a bite of lunch in the cafeteria. He'd missed his lunch appointment with the chief accountant, but maybe he could catch her, unobserved, and warn her. It wouldn't take much. She'd ask what happened to him. He'd say two men tried to snatch his briefcase on Grand Avenue, as he walked between buildings. The same conversation he'd had with about a dozen people already.

\* \* \*

In the Personnel Director's office the direct line on Hartig's desk rang with two short, jarring bursts, a precursor to the message. Jake stabbed at the speakerphone, ensuring it was off.

"This is Jake."

A demanding male voice delivered carefully selected phrases. "Our friend has gone to lunch, but perhaps he left a message for you in his office. We need to close the deal, so don't waste any time. No one is around who can help you at the moment."

"Why me?" Jake asked to the dial tone.

Nettle must have had his finger on the button to cut off any protest. Who does he think he is?

Jake's chest tightened. Angry thoughts swirled in his mind, but he pushed himself out of the black leather chair and headed for the corner offices which commanded the more spectacular views of Lake Merritt.

The President's office and executive conference room had a curved glass wall covering 180 degrees. The windows looked out upon the Bay Bridge and Treasure Island at the west, to Lake Merritt and the Oakland Hills to the east. But Jake wasn't going to the President's office, nor was he the least bit interested in the views. He passed a second palatial office and stopped at the third door. This office also had a spectacular view, but was small and spartan by comparison to the first two. The furniture was expensive, Swedish, comfortable, but not for too long, except for the cream colored, high back leather chair behind the desk. Hartig wiped away the perspiration beading on his upper lip and forehead.

Jake tapped lightly on the glass partition separating the secretaries' work area from the passageway. Next, he casually glanced into the reception area to be sure all the secretaries gone. At least Shade had been right about the offices' being empty.

Jake could see Shade Nettle had stationed himself at the end of the corridor where he could easily watch the closest bank of elevators, and see across most of the inner office partitions.

Appearing nonchalant, Shade fiddled with an unlit cigarette. Smoking was prohibited in the building.

Creep. How's he going to warn me if Steadhold shows up? Jake wondered. What am I supposed to find anyway, some tidy memo right on Steadhold's desk? The guy's got nothing on us.

Jake quickly entered Roger's office, saw the scratched briefcase on the small, round conference table, squeezed his eyes shut a moment and decided to start there. He forced the lock with Roger's brass letter opener, scratching it, and thumbed through the papers. He found computer printouts, generated in Accounting, lots of them, going back two to three years. How much did Steadhold suspect?

Three years — Damn! Does it go back that far? Wonder if the time frame will mean something more to Nettle? If so, what's he pulling?

He did see some "cannot verify" notations and the initials. There was nothing else unusual. Some of the documents were the detailed backup for the upcoming stockholders meeting, all very mundane. Maybe the time frame was coincidental. He also found some spreadsheets; data generated on a PC, probably either the one on Steadhold's desk or one he had at home. Again, nothing out of the ordinary, so far as he could tell, no unusual runs of figures, losses or account codes. Hartig had no head for figures, and he couldn't take the runs. They would be missed. He returned the papers to the briefcase and tried to close the broken latch. The neat little stack of things Roger had taken from his jacket attracted Jake's attention next, handkerchief, green notebook and a parking validation. He flipped through the notebook and saw the familiar name of Al Gonzales. It might be useful to get to this troublemaker someday. He scribbled the name, address and telephone number quickly inside his pocket date book. Jake's thoughts jumbled as he moved.

So, Steadhold wants me to hire this guy — hardly. My two hired friends might want to settle with Mr. Gonzales. Nothing else on the desktop.

He opened the side drawers and went though each quickly, nothing. Nettle must be crazy. He left the office and looked for Nettle, but he was gone.

Great, just great. Was he going to warn me, or set me up?

Back in his own office, Jake yanked open his desk drawer and raked the contents with his fingers until he found his Valium. Unscrewing the cap, he stared in disbelief when only one tablet dropped into his palm. He noted that he had no more refills on the prescription, and threw the container into his trashcan with such force that it circled the rim and bounced onto the carpet. He slumped into his chair, drew several deep breaths, and dialed his therapist's office.

When Roger returned from lunch, he failed to notice his briefcase and the green notebook had been moved. He was short on time. The secretaries were still gone on their walk. Later, when he did notice the broken lock, he attributed it to the day's events.

\* \* \*

At three fifteen, Shade Nettle was disappointed to find Jake's secretary, Alice, at her desk during the normal afternoon break. He recovered, fancying himself effective with women.

"Hi. What a surprise. Don't you look lovely today, Alice, like a ray of sunshine. When are you going to teach me that sexy tango?" Nettle bulldozed ahead, not interested in a response. "I thought I'd drop in on Jake. If he's free for a moment."

"I'll let him know you're here." She smiled and rang her boss, but Shade nodded to Jake through the glass, and Jake waved him inside.

"Go right in," said Alice. "Will you be needing anything? If not, I think I'll take my break. I'm starting to slip on all the oil around here."

This time she smiled so sweetly that Nettle only briefly thought Alice might have been referring to him. She left, and he went into Hartig's office and closed the door.

"The incompetence of you and your 'connections' is mind numbing. How in the hell did they —. Oh, forget it. Did you find anything in his office?"

"The printouts he has go back three years, Shade. Have you been screwing with me?"

Nettle flopped into a chair, which creaked under his sudden weight. He blew away Hartig's assertion. "Probably pulling in all kinds of data for a fishing expedition. Doesn't know where to begin. Where is it? Let's have a look."

"I left it. He'd miss it."

"He'd miss it? Of course, he would miss it! Why do you think we wanted that briefcase? You're an idiot."

"You told me to see what he had. You didn't say to take anything."

Shade sighed. "We won't get another chance like that one. Could you tell when the data were generated?"

"What do you mean?"

"Was there a date on the top of the page? Any of the pages? Any handwritten notes anywhere?"

"Just the dates of the line items all in sequence, nothing to tell me when the stuff was generated. There were some 'cannot verify' notations in pen."

"Jake, we can't afford to have Steadhold stumble onto our little operation. We'll swing as high for twenty thousand as we would for a million. Doesn't seem fair, does it?"

"I could arrange for him to disappear."

"Could you, now. The same guys who loused up snatching the briefcase?"

"That was a fluke. Bad luck. It won't happen again."

Shade clawed at his hairline with his fingernails and rubbed his forehead, trying to think. Jake pushed ahead. "I'll need some cash. They only work for cash."

"Use part of the ten thou I gave you. It couldn't possibly be gone this fast. We'll settle up when our problem is solved."

Silence.

Nettle stood up. "Oh, Jake, if something goes wrong this time. Take his wife."

"What?"

"Carol Steadhold. If there's another screw-up, don't simply look around. Tell 'em to take his wife, if she's all they can get. We'll get him that way."

Five minutes later, Nettle returned to his office, red-faced, pounding his fist into his left hand, his mind racing. Three years of records from Accounting, the time probably not coincidental, but without the exact runs, how can I know? Steadhold has got to go and go fast, then when the timing is right, Jake too.

Busy with other matters in the afternoon, and with his mind functioning on two levels, Shade Nettle became increasingly anxious. He would need to move up his timetable. Nonetheless, he took time for some trivia.

Late that night, in the records department at city hall, Jake Hartig's condo had a contractor's lien placed on it for remodeling work never reimbursed. Shade used a valid license number from one contractor with the name of another. Jake would learn of it only if he tried to sell the property. That kind of glitch would take years to correct.

*       *       *

Jimmy had never been an inmate at the main county jail, only in juvie, and he didn't like it. His yellow blond hair hung in scraggly uneven locks, not long, but unkempt. The bruises on his face and arms told of his recent efforts to steal Roger Steadhold's briefcase. He looked up anxiously when a jailer appeared.

"Hey, You. James Thrasher, assault and battery — attempted theft. Bail's been posted. Come with me."

Some little bald guy he thought was Adenhauer bailed him out of jail and disappeared before Jimmy could even thank him. He caught just a brief glance, but it looked like Adenhauer. Outside, Jimmy found a pay phone and called the number he had memorized. No answer. He went home to his untidy, one room cave of an apartment and tried again from the pay phone down the hall. Adenhauer had said to use pay phones.

"Say, what about the court date, man?"

"You screw up once more, and you're on your own. Understand? You are to do exactly as you're told. No changes. When you're working for us you don't pee, unless you're told to. Got it? I'll meet you guys tomorrow, same time and place as last time."

"The court date," Jimmy repeated, but the connection was broken.

Jake Hartig hung up his telephone and checked his messages. The pharmacy had called. His new prescription was ready. Prozac, this time.

# Chapter 6

From twenty stories above, the people walking along the wide sidewalks of the plaza area looked small, inconsequential. The plaza in front of the main entrance to Canby International Headquarters was a gathering place. More people than usual for mid-afternoon, however, headed into the building through the massive glass and chrome doors.

Prior to the Canby annual stockholders meeting at two p.m., the Steadholds and the Nettles had lunch together. The Nettles had suggested it. Insisted, actually. The four of them chatted and walked rapidly towards the normally spectacular fountain, now shut off because of the drought. Angie Nettle wore a white sharkskin suit. Carol Steadhold was dressed in electric blue. The couples were easy to spot from the twentieth floor, if anyone was watching.

"Out!" Jake Hartig said to his secretary, without taking his eyes off the scene below him. "Out! I'm busy!" He waved his hand in a disgusted, angry sweep toward the door.

"Certainly, sir." Alice closed the door and shook her head. "Yeah, right. Wish I could get *paid* for staring out the window."

Alone inside his office the personnel director was smiling now, a perverse, one-sided smile, while he watched the arranged production far below.

At first only Carol noticed a man with his small camera pointed in their direction. With his shirttails untucked and his wrinkled pants baggy at the ankles, he had a disheveled appearance, but he was watching them. She glared at him as the camera flashed. The four of them overtook two women walking more slowly and the camera flashed again.

Carol stopped. "That man is taking our picture."

"I saw a flash," said Angie, slowing.

The man moved on casually, passing them as he tucked his camera into his shirt pocket. Steadhold and Nettle glanced up but continued their pace. "Must be a tourist," said Roger.

"Doesn't look like a tourist." Carol turned to follow the others.

"Maybe he's homeless." Angie Nettle stopped. "Look at him."

The man ambled down the sidewalk. Shade and Roger barely paused to glance in the direction she indicated.

"I've heard that some people take pictures of strangers and use them for making false identification documents," Angie said.

Shade took Roger's arm and increased his pace. "Today's announcement of the split should make the stockholders even happier. Evert will be announcing the worst kept secret in the company. The wire service carried the news this morning."

"Yeah, I heard it," said Roger. "Evert's secretary tells me you have a real razzle-dazzle of a presentation for today, all kinds of color graphics." They continued to talk, moving up the low steps and through the gleaming portico. Several steps back, Carol and Angie followed.

At one of the hors d'oeuvre tables after the speeches, Roger nearly bumped into Shona Oliver, the chief accountant, slicing menacingly into the flower decorated wheel of Brie. Her back was turned to him as he approached the jumbo shrimp. She had missed him at the roast beef, but guessed correctly that either the sushi or the shrimp would be his next target.

Shona glanced from the table to Roger and back at the table again, appearing to be interested in the food. "I'm taking a leave. Just got it approved. Be gone four weeks. The company thinks I'm visiting my sick mother in Nevada. I'll be with a friend in LA, if you need to get in touch. I've sent my number to your home address. Better alert your wife." A little, nervous laugh escaped from her mouth and she moved away. Roger took some shrimp.

Discarding the Brie, Shona moved to the end of the table, took a fresh plate, selected two chocolate dipped strawberries, and joined some office friends. Her eyes casually roamed the huge room. She watched as Roger dipped one of the shrimp into the spicy, red cocktail sauce and bit into it. She didn't know him well, but Hsing Tom had trusted him.

Across the room, she saw Carol catch her husband's eye and nod covertly at one of the founders standing alone with his flute of champagne. Shona Oliver observed Roger nod back to his wife and the smiling Carol move to engage the founder in a brief conversation. Shona had never studied a politician in action and was interested in how Carol purposefully moved through the crowd, greeting, chatting, making eye contact and smiling mysteriously when someone asked her about higher office. But Carol Steadhold was not the person who transferred Hsing to Taipei. Where was Nettle?

There he was, in conversation with Jake Hartig by the windows in the corner. Evert Johns, with two board members in tow, beckoned Nettle. Hartig followed to join the cluster around the striking CEO, with his full head of white, neatly trimmed hair. Barrel-chested, gray-eyed Evert Johns had the handshake and style of a man who missed very little and had no tolerance for fools. Shona knew that Johns could charm anyone, but he only indulged in serious conversation with those whom he felt were worthy. Shona also noted that Evert Johns, having connected the board members with Nettle, excused himself from the group and joined another. Carol Steadhold wasn't the only one making the rounds.

Following the reception, Carol dropped Angie Nettle off at her Elizabethan mansion in Piedmont and continued on her way home to Danville. Angie had talked incessantly, thrilled with the prospect of redoing the gun room into a proper drawing room since Shade had decided to ship his gun collection to an uncle in Switzerland. Carol was thankful for the time alone. She saw the first tentacles of fog probing the hills, cooling the Oakland/Berkeley side, promising the valley cooler temperatures, if the fog could scale this section of the coastal range. She drove through the Caldacott Tunnel, through Orinda and Lafayette to Walnut Creek, turning onto Highway 680, past Alamo and finally to Danville. Traffic was heavy. Exhaust fumes worked their way into the car, but she remained preoccupied by the man with the camera, thinking it was odd, very odd.

Several days later, at twelve forty-seven a.m., an e-mail message sent from an eastbound 737 was transmitted for Roger Steadhold, who would not see it for several hours.

Roger, Need you to go to New York on first available flight. Janet will have a report for you this a.m. Take as much time as necessary to solve any problems and make a full assessment. In addition, please investigate the new business prospects mentioned in the report.

Also need you to drop by the service support office in Boston if everything in New York works out and there is time.

I have alerted Janet and Phyllis to this change in schedule and asked them to make the necessary travel and accommodation arrangements. Have a good trip.

Sorry for the short notice, but the timing is important.

Evert

A week earlier, Diane Lind received a telephone call from Sacramento. It was the director of California Elected Women, Evelyn Day. The unity meeting among the representatives of the governmental agencies had been a good effort. Evelyn wanted a further follow-up, in several areas, and asked Diane, an officer in both California Elected Women and the California School Boards' Association, to arrange a meeting among the top people. The objective was to formalize a closer working relationship between the California School Boards Association and CEW.

Evelyn said, "One of the things I need every year is access to the updated lists of women school board members. If they could generate the mailing labels for us, that would be best. If you make the initial contacts, I'll follow up and arrange a dinner meeting at the Capitol Club here in Sacramento, just the five of us."

"Sure. Where's the Capitol Club?"

"It's at the top of the Darth Vader building — that's an irreverent description we use up here. I'll get you the address.

"The black building with the inverted triangles on top? Okay. By the way, I know we've had our unity meeting and all, but there're still tensions among the various governmental entities, even with the May Revise numbers looking better than the original budget projections."

"You think they won't attend?" asked Evelyn.

"They'll attend. No harm in talking. Just that there'll be certain undercurrents. Carol's our president, but she also represents cities, and we don't have a state budget yet."

"I'll keep that in mind."

Carol and Diane drove up to Sacramento together. The air in the state capitol was hot, dry, and charged with static and rumors on the evening of their dinner meeting. Legislative leaders negotiated with the governor's office and each other, trying to pass a budget on time, sensing the possible, but knowing they would probably miss the deadline, again. Compared to what was going on around them, the dinner meeting was delightful. Initial tensions melted to simple alertness, most apparent when the school board association's top lobbyist came in with an urgent, private message for his director.

The two directors exchanged thoughts about corporate sponsors and the fact that California Elected Women had a policy of paying certain expenses, but no honoraria to conference speakers. Diane and the others were aware that they discussed these innocent topics while the future financial state of their agencies was traded back and forth among champions and detractors a few blocks away.

# Chapter 7

The warm July Tuesday was one of those early mornings that inspired visitors to California to stay forever. The coastal hills had turned to gold, but in places, live oaks majestically defied the drought with their dark green canopies. Diane enjoyed seeing the huge, graceful trees clustering in the crevices and the arroyos of the hills. Along the highway, just before she dropped into the Sunol Valley, she spotted two deer in the shadows.

Diane liked driving to Sacramento with Carol. They had become good friends, and the trip always seemed faster when they went together. Of course, coming from Cupertino, Diane was about halfway there by the time she reached Danville. Today Diane would leave her car in Danville, and Carol would drive to Sacramento. The CEW officers would meet at the county governments' association offices, downtown, but California Elected Women was headquartered at Sacramento State University.

Born out of the frustration of earlier elected women in California, when their numbers were smaller, the organization had grown from a support group into an important education and research organization in partnership with the University. CEW's goal was to promote and support more women in seeking public office and positions on statewide boards and commissions.

In Danville, Diane turned off the highway at Diablo Road and continued the short distance to the town hall. She pulled into the small parking lot, and parked next to Carol's car. Inside, the receptionist offered Diane a cup of coffee while she waited. The mayor was on the phone. Diane declined the coffee, but did take advantage of the delay to find the restroom. It was ten minutes more before Carol appeared.

"I need to run by the house for just a second. I have to leave some instructions for our new gardener. It's not far," she said as they headed for the parking lot.

"Fine, we should have plenty of time."

"Roger was going to write out the instructions for the gardener, but he was called into the office on an emergency early this morning, and after he got there, he phoned to tell me he was leaving for New York. It's a good thing he decided to keep a change of clothes downtown after he was mugged. He'll have to buy anything else he needs.

"I was talking with the mayors of Kentfield and Pinole this morning," Carol said, changing the subject. "What do you know about Senate Bill 797? Isn't Becky Morgan your senator?"

"Well, I'm on her education advisory committee, and we met with her two weeks ago. I don't recognize SB 797 off the top of my head. What is it?"

"It's her regional government proposal, and to be honest, I don't think it's very well thought out."

"Oh, yes, I am familiar with the bill. Becky did mention it as one of the things she's been pushing. It's a limited regional approach, as I understand it, merging the Air Quality Board with the Transportation Commission and the Association of Bay Area Governments in an effort to coordinate regional planning. She definitely plans to pursue it."

"There are a number of cities that have real problems with it," Carol said.

"You mean it's a lot like the 'quick fix' proposals to consolidate all the school districts?" Diane asked. "Seems like a great idea to people who haven't taken the time to study the issues involved."

Carol cocked her head to one side ever so slightly and smiled out of one corner of her mouth. Diane got into Carol's car. Time to go to a subject on which they could agree.

Diane had been thinking about the composition of CEW's board of directors and the changes that could come with the November elections. The two women pulled out of the town hall parking lot, took the first right, drove about a mile, turned right again past a small, dried up apricot orchard.

"Apricots do better on my side of the Bay," Diane said absently. They drove by a black van parked in the dirt at the edge of the orchard. A scraggly-looking man leaned out of the window. He wore a black baseball cap, black tee shirt and held a transceiver in his left hand, resting at the open window. They both saw him.

"Someone putting in a pool?" asked Diane.

"What?"

"Once, I noticed a strange man with a transceiver in my neighborhood. It was someone on the construction crew, calling in the trucks with the heavy equipment for putting in a swimming pool."

"Think I'll call the sheriff when we get to the house, just to be sure the neighbors aren't about to lose all their possessions," said Carol.

The conversation returned to CEW and the fact that the legislator who was vice president had decided not to run again for her seat in the Assembly. It might confuse the succession to the presidency, and they needed to double-check the bylaws. They were discussing who would be best to add to the executive board as Carol pulled into her curved driveway and stopped the car.

"Come on in. I'll try to hurry."

Carol quickly unlocked the front door, left it open and disappeared into the house.

"I'm going to check the phone messages before I write that note for the gardener," she called over her shoulder, "since Roger won't be coming home."

Diane followed leisurely. In the foyer, she called out, "How about Marian, Carol?"

"Who?"

"Marian Regal. Alameda County supervisor."

The sudden thud and crash of heavy coat hangers inside the hall closet startled her. Diane wheeled around towards the sound.

"Carol, something's in your —." Her lips moved, but there was no further sound. The closet door had opened. Her eyes fixed on the gun pointed right at her. A latex glove covered the hand holding it.

Carol immediately came to see what was wrong. The man said nothing, just herded them to one corner with short, jabbing motions of the gun. In his left hand he held a transceiver up to his mouth.

"Rudy, bring the van up here."

"Nobody in a white Taurus has come by yet."

"We got a problem. Get up here. The guy ain't comin'."

Pointing the gun directly at Carol's heart, the intruder continued matter-of-factly.

"Okay, where's Roger? He was supposed to be here this mornin'."

I'm tripling my contributions to Handgun Control, Carol told herself. The thought comforted her, and her composure began to return. Her eyes darted to Diane and back to the gun. Diane's expression was one of confusion and consternation, but there was no panic. It would not do to challenge this man's assumptions or to appear any way other than submissive. She kept her eyes on the gun and tried to look frightened. It was easy.

"Where's Roger?" The man moved the gun slowly and deliberately to point at the middle of Carol's face.

After a pause, she understood the question.

"He's catching a plane for New York at ten." She spoke to the gun.

"He's not coming back here?"

"Not today."

"When?"

"Probably several days. It's business. He wasn't sure."

"How long did he know about this trip?"

"What?"

"When did he know he was going on a trip? I don't believe you."

But he did believe her, Carol felt. His voice had seemed to change slightly. She could hear his anger and desperation.

Diane forced herself to study him. His blue eyes were set close to the bony bridge of his nose, his blond hair limp and uneven, small ears close to his skull. Yellow and purple traces encircled the left side of his face and the right lower chin. Thin and about her height, he reminded her of a raptor.

Carol said, "He got a call this morning very early and went right in, then he called me from the office after he got to work. It's some sort of an emergency in New York." Carol heard her own words tumbling out with odd little high pitches. Phony fear, well, maybe not so phony. She was still talking to the gun, her eyes wide.

"Let's go to the garage. Get your purse." He jerked the gun indicating the direction. Carol led the way. Diane followed. Going through the kitchen, the gunman picked up Carol's purse and replaced the telephone receiver which was askew and making noises. In the garage, he pressed the garage door opener and it rose to reveal Carol's silver BMW in the driveway with a black van pulling along side. It had a small Chevrolet insignia on the front grille and the two large mirrors on the either side. The driver turned off the motor but stayed in the vehicle. Don't go to a secondary location, raced through Carol's mind, but she didn't know what else to do.

"Keep an eye on things," the gunman spoke into his radio. "I'll have her put the car inside."

56

A movement caught his eye. Suddenly the dog door banged open and a very excited Schnauzer burst into the garage from the back yard.

"Whiskers!" Carol said, involuntarily.

The little dog seemed beside himself with joy, jumping and leaping up on all three of them, but he especially circled around Carol. Silent before he entered the garage, Whiskers now yelped, barked and danced excitedly. The gunman kicked at the dog, missed. He put down his radio and pulled a cylinder from his pocket.

Oh, my God, thought Carol. Diane also recognized the silencer. Whiskers was winding down, however, since the people weren't paying any attention to him. He raced out to the driveway, stopped for only a brief backward look at his mistress and took off through the front yard and down the street. The women each took a deep breath. The gunman showed no emotion. The silencer was in place.

"Get your car keys." He grabbed Carol's purse and threw it at her. She pulled out her keys.

"Nice and normal-like, walk back there and hand your purse to the driver. Take her's too. Then get into your car and pull it into the garage."

She did as he ordered. Diane saw her walking slowly, probably hoping a neighbor would drive by and see her predicament, but no one did. Handing the purses into the open van window, Carol realized another gun pointed at her. The man in black held it even with his chest, pointed directly at her.

"Just drop 'em in my lap."

She dropped the purses and went around the front of her car and got in. Diane watched her. Carol thought of Whiskers running freely around the neighborhood. She knew she should slam the car into reverse and race away. The man in the garage held his gun higher, aimed at her head, as if reading her thoughts. Carol started the car and edged it slowly into the garage, turned it off and got out. I should have gone for it. Right when I started the car. I should have slammed that thing in reverse and gone for it.

The gunman in the garage gave more orders. "Get those burlap sacks and that duct tape." Diane picked up the hefty, rough sacks used for curbside recycling, and looked around for the duct tape. "Dump 'em out first."

"Jimmy, We don't want that other woman. Leave her inside, where the body won't be seen," the radio crackled.

"We're no good to you. You don't want us," Diane said softly.

"They've seen us," the man in the van muttered not using the radio. "Shoot her."

Jimmy grabbed Diane's arm and shoved her. "Go to the van. The side door. You, too."

"We only want the wife, Jimmy. We got a big enough problem with one."

"Hey, this gives us a little more time, that's all. Just shut up and keep your gun on them." ·

Rudy's eyes narrowed. He undid his seatbelt and made a move toward the open side door, but stopped. He kept his gun pointed at them.

The women watched in disbelief as the first man tucked his gun away and pulled out two narrow plastic strips. He fastened Carol's hands behind her back with a long, self-locking tie, flexcuffs. This is it. We're dead, Carol thought. Then it was Diane's turn.

Jimmy yanked Carol's arm and shoved her onto the floor of the van behind the second row of seats. Diane started screaming. Jimmy slapped her hard, breaking her glasses and sending them to the pavement. He then tore a strip of duct tape and pushing Diane's head against the seat, slapped her twice more, then pressed the tape roughly across her mouth. Carol received similar treatment.

To secure their feet, he used a large, orange extension cord, from the garage, looping it around the bottom of one of the seats.

"No noise and no movin' around. None. You got that? I said, You got that?"

The women nodded, not meeting his eyes. Jimmy pulled the scratchy, burlap sacks over their heads and upper bodies.

"Lie down. Don't move once we get goin'."

The women did as he demanded. He rolled them roughly toward the back and threw a ratty blanket over their legs and feet. When he appeared satisfied that they were innocuous-looking bumps on the floor, he joined his companion in the front.

"Sure hope you know what you're doin'," said Rudy, twisting the steering wheel. "Get the garage door opener out of her car."

Jimmy retrieved it. The garage door closed, and they drove down the street at twenty-five miles an hour. Turning the corner, the driver slowed even more for Jimmy to roll down his window and fling the garage door opener as far as he could into the orchard. It landed in a weedy clump. Rudy switched on the van's radio and adjusted the speakers so the sound came from the back and would make it hard for the captives to overhear them.

Inside their sacks, the women were increasingly hot and uncomfortable. Coarse burlap scratched and dug into their faces and now there was the assault of junk radio, a station blaring rude commentary solely for its shock value. Carol tried to remember the number and direction of the turns they took, but she quickly became disoriented. The awful station did state the time occasionally, their one link to reality. The men talked in agitated whispers.

"We'll pick up the car, go to the boat, then dump this van and follow the plan. I'll call and explain and get instructions." Jimmy said. "It's a little different situation. That's all."

"You freakin' idiot! Now I know why they call you guys idiots. You shouda shot the dame and left her inside."

"We can still do it. The boat's a better place. Nobody'll look there. It's no big deal. Who says we even have to tell Adenhauer?"

59

"Yeah? Well, we better tell him. I can hear it now. Got a little bonus for you — the Steadhold dame an' some other dame too. That's not his real name, you know."

"Sure it is, I saw it on the mailbox."

"Not Steadhold. Adenhauer, asshole."

"Hey, we've done lots of jobs for Adenhauer."

"Only two and it was little stuff. Nothin' like kidnapping someone, man. What happened at the house, anyway? I warned you. Couldn't you hide somewhere or something?" Rudy asked.

"Just shut up. I hid in the closet. Damn that Marian Regal. How can one bitch cause so much misery in my life?"

"I don't know what you're talking about. Just shut up. We need to do some hard thinking. Let's do what we planned, but we've got to make some extra plans now."

"We didn't make the first plans. Adenhauer did."

"We'd better start thinkin' for ourselves."


Whiskers returned, sniffed nervously at the garage door and then meandered up to the front entrance and began sniffing at the front door. It was not closed tightly. He jumped up and pushed on it with his front feet. It opened enough to let him squeeze inside. After wandering through the empty house, the dog hopped onto the forbidden white sofa and stretched out for a nap.

# Chapter 8

In the small, 1920's era bungalow on Humbolt Street in east Oakland, Al Gonzales put some plums in a paper bag for his lunch, grabbed the map to the Steadhold's, and went out to his car. With the help of a neighbor, he had the old Dodge Dart running again. The Tribune had run the story of the attempted robbery and how Al had helped capture the assailant. The Casper's manager called Al and offered him a part time position. His job at Casper's didn't pay much, but he wouldn't go hungry.

Mr. Steadhold had offered him a job, too. Not the one Al had dreamed of with Canby International, but it was work, and he liked gardening. Mr. Steadhold had discussed his working one full day a week and that everything to do with the yard would be his responsibility. Al liked the idea of making decisions on supplies and being a trusted employee, and he appreciated the way Mr. Steadhold talked to him, man-to-man, rather than big boss to laborer. He wondered how Mrs. Steadhold would be, but he wasn't worried because Mr. Steadhold was so decent. He even had advanced Al the first month's salary, correctly sensing his financial plight.

Al took pride in his small, one bedroom bungalow, broken front steps, peeling paint and all. His landlord, Old Lady Frances, would let him fix up things as he could and reduce the rent accordingly, but until recently, he hadn't had much time for house repairs.

Finding the Steadhold house in Danville after only a couple of wrong turns, Al parked and headed for the garden shed around back. The shed was larger than his living room. It had a cement floor, two windows, shelves, a deep sink and tools neatly arranged, even a telephone. He made a mental note to remember to replace each tool in its place, and looked around on the counter area for the note Mr. Steadhold said he would leave. Finding none, he decided to do the obvious things.

He examined the lawn mower, checked the gas and started to work. After the lawn, there was edging and weeding to be done. Al dug out a couple of overgrown sprinklers in the front lawn and was trimming the small hedge lining the walk when he noticed the front door was ajar. He rang the bell and thought he heard a low sound and quick scurrying. That was all, no other sound. He rang again and stuck his head inside.

"Mr. Steadhold? Mrs. Steadhold?"

He stepped inside feeling very uneasy.

"Mr. Steadhold? Mrs. Steadhold?"

Nothing. The entryway closet door was open and three large, wooden hangers were on the tile floor of the foyer. He decided to walk through quickly, very quickly, to be sure everything was all right. He went fast, just glancing into each room. A tiny movement of the lace dust ruffle on the bed in the master bedroom caused him to look again. A lump rose in his throat.

"Mr. Steadhold?"

It moved again! He wasn't imagining it. He moved cautiously and bent down on one knee. With a sudden jerk, he lifted the ruffle and Al peered right into Whiskers' furry face. Whiskers zoomed straight out the far side, tail first. Al had never seen a dog do that. He started laughing, his anxiety relieved by this ridiculous, backwards scooting dog.

Al had seen the sturdy doghouse and the small dog dishes in the fenced backyard, but he had forgotten them until now. His relieved, loud laugh did little to reassure Whiskers, however. The dog was cornered and began barking a high pitched, nervous bark. Al stopped laughing and began talking to the dog gently and gave him more space. Whiskers responded by growling.

Al began to walk out of the room, still talking to the dog. Fortunately, the Milk Bones were out on the kitchen counter and when Al offered one to Whiskers, the two became friends. Al picked up the dog and the box of treats and went out the front door, taking care to lock it behind him. Inside the back gate, he put the dog down.

"There you go, little fella. I'll get you some fresh water and leave these for you." He filled the second dish with small, multi-colored Milk Bones and put the box in the garden house — he couldn't think of it as a shed. At the sight of the telephone, Al decided it would be a good idea to call Mr. Steadhold. Things were a little strange. He pulled his direction sheet from his pocket and tapped in the number.

"Mr. Steadhold's office."

"Ah, hi. This is Al Gonzales, his new gardener. I need to talk to Mr. Steadhold, please."

"Oh, hello, Mr. Gonzales. I know who you are. I'm Phyllis. Mr. Steadhold told me about how you helped him catch that mugger. Unfortunately, he had to fly to New York this morning. Can I help in any way?"

"Well, I thought he should know that I found the front door open and his dog inside. I've locked the door and put the dog in the backyard. It didn't look like anything was wrong, just the door left ajar. I'm calling from the garden house phone."

"The house is locked now?"

"Yeah, and the dog's outside. He has a house and run outside, in the back."

"That sounds fine, Mr. Gonzales. I think I'll call the Danville town hall to see if I can reach Mrs. Steadhold and let her know too. Thank you very much."

She flipped through her file for the number and called. At town hall, the receptionist told her the mayor had left for Sacramento, but said she would put her through to the city manager. Phyllis told the city manager what the new gardener had found and that Roger would be gone for a few days. The city manager said he would see to it. He arose, called back Deputy Sheriff Dennis McClatchy, who had just left his office, explained, and asked him if he could check on the Steadhold house.

"Sure thing," said McClatchy, glancing at his watch. "If I can get a copy of this waiver application to take with me, I'm almost finished here. I can go right over on my way back to Walnut Creek. I don't need to be at the high school until twelve twenty to speak to the afternoon classes."

Al was continuing his inspection of the grounds for things that needed to be done. The sound of cicadas alerted him to the fact that the fruit trees would have some dead limbs in the fall and would need careful pruning and disposal of the dead branches. The borers were hard on trees.

At eleven thirty, he stopped and ate his plums under Whiskers' close scrutiny.

"You aren't hungry or you would have eaten all those little doggy biscuits I gave you."

A car drove up the driveway. Whiskers started barking importantly, except that his short tail was wagging too. Al left him and went to see who was there.

"Hi, I understand you found the front door open this morning," said Deputy McClatchy, extending his hand.

"Yeah, I did. I thought I'd better lock it. No one's home. I took the dog out. Looks like they keep him outside."

"Have you seen anyone around here? Anyone at all this morning or notice anything else unusual?"

"No, but it's my first day on the job. Mr. Steadhold was supposed to leave me some instructions, but his office said he had to go on an emergency trip. I called his secretary when I found the door to the house open. I did go inside because I heard a noise. It turned out to be the dog, hiding under the bed. I brought him out. Oh, there are some big coat hangers on the floor near the front door. Otherwise, things look in order."

"Okay, thanks very much. I'll take a look around."

Circling the house, McClatchy found nothing unusual, except in looking through the window of the side door into the double garage, he noticed a car and some empty cans on the floor of the otherwise neat garage. He noticed the dog door built into the outside door and assumed the dog had gotten into some trash. He stood over some black tire marks on the cement driveway, wheels turned in place. On the way back to his patrol car he spotted a roll of duct tape under a bottle brush bush beside the driveway and a pair of broken glasses. He picked them up and took them to Al.

"What can you tell me about these?"

Al took the roll of tape and the glasses and handed them back. "Nothing. Where were they?"

"Can I see some identification?"

"Sure. This is my first day on the job. Got here about ten fifteen. Nobody's been around. Only met Mr. Steadhold once. Real nice guy. I've never met Mrs. Steadhold."

Deputy McClatchy noted Al's address and telephone number. "Been here since ten fifteen? Did you notice anything strange when you arrived, other than the door open? Anyone see you arrive?"

In his car on the way to Walnut Creek McClatchy called Danville town hall. The city manager had gone to lunch. It was nearly four before he was able to call again. He was behind on his regular work. He tapped his fingers as he waited for the call to go through.

"I went by the Steadholds' this morning. There are a couple of worrisome things. Her car is in the garage, and I thought they were both out of town," he told the city manager.

"Oh, well, I know that Carol was going to drive up to Sacramento with another woman. She was here this morning. They probably took the other woman's car."

65

"Possibly. I found a pair of broken glasses, a roll of tape and some stuff spilled on the garage floor. What do you know about the new gardener they have? When is the mayor due back, tonight?

"The gardener is a fellow who helped Roger Steadhold fight off a mugger. And, yes, Carol's due back by tonight."

"Someone needs to check to see that she's home this evening. It's probably nothing, but you never know."

# Chapter 9

Diane tried to stay calm, but she could feel panic around the edges of her thoughts. She kept fighting to push it back. Her burlap cocoon was hot and scratchy. Exhaust fumes occasionally seeped in. Nausea threatened with every turn or bump in the road. One nostril clogged. She had allergies. There were stops, stop signs or signals. They realized they must be off the freeway, but where?

Diane told herself to stay strong for Carol, that Carol would stay strong for her.

Panic now shot into her mind like laser streaks, cutting through her resolve. She tried to mentally push back the shafts of white fear when she remembered that two years earlier, a woman in Cupertino had died in a similar situation. An intruder had bound and gagged the victim with duct tape, and she had suffocated. Diane began to squirm. Her heart raced. Her breathing labored through the open nostril.

She prayed and told herself, Stay calm. Stay calm.

\*   \*   \*

Jimmy went through both women's purses, taking all the cash, studying the pictures, the membership and medical insurance cards, which he left. "Did you know the Steadhold woman is a mayor? Won't a lot of people know her?"

"No shit? Mayor of Danville?" said Rudy. "Well, it's no big deal. All these little towns have mayors. Not like Oakland where they elect a mayor for four years, and everybody knows who he is. These little places rotate the job every year so everyone gets a turn. I doubt half the people in her town know who the mayor is."

"The other one's president of some school district board of trustees," Jimmy said.

"Who cares?"

"How'd you know all that, about mayors?" asked Jimmy.

"I read the papers. And I didn't drop out of school like you did."

Jimmy shrugged and counted out the cash, two hundred twenty-six dollars. He gave half to Rudy, who folded it in a wad and stuffed it in his shirt pocket as he drove. Jimmy kept the coins. Rudy hated to be bothered with change. Jimmy's thoughts went back to trying to figure out how things went wrong. Early on, everything had gone perfectly.

He had played the role of a customer at the Dodge place in Pleasanton. He went back into the work area on the pretext of discussing a number of problems with the service manager and took the first van he found, an older black Chevy. Surprisingly, the keys had been tucked above the visor. Driving away, he had marveled that it had been so simple. He didn't have to use any of the excuses he had ready. He'd simply told the service representative he had forgotten his cigarettes and drove out right by the guy as he talked to someone else.

After the fiasco in Oakland, when he tried to act like a homeless person to steal the briefcase, it had been a relief to pull off stealing the van so smoothly. But kidnapping two women instead of the man they wanted was bad.

"You figure five p.m. before they miss the van?" Rudy asked.

"Yeah, that was the easiest part of this whole mess. We could ditch it in Tracy instead of Livermore, if you want. It's not as far to drive."

"Nah, we better stick to the original plan. Tracy is too close to the boat."

"When should we call Adenhauer, or whatever you think his name is?"

Rudy scratched his stringy beard, then picked his nose. Jimmy knew he probably was thinking and waited. But Rudy stayed silent so Jimmy began again.

"What if he's ticked when he finds out we have two old dames instead of Steadhold?"

"Snatching his wife was the back-up plan. We did that. He'll probably want 'em both disappeared."

"Disappeared?"

"Killed. Out of sight, man. Got any better ideas? Like running into traffic with that briefcase, getting beat up and thrown into jail? Geez."

"You ever killed anyone, Rudy?"

Everyone bragged about doing some drivebys or other stuff, but Jimmy had never killed or seriously hurt anyone. Broke one guy's arm, he reminded himself.

"Nah, but I was there when Manuel got it," Rudy answered after a slight hesitation.

"Manuel?"

"Remember, the guy from school."

"Oh, Manny." Jimmy glanced away. His index finger began hopping up and down on his knee.

Rudy thought some more, picked his nose again and then cleaned his fingernail with his teeth.

"Maybe this is too big a job for us, Jimmy." Rudy seemed to have a change of heart. "We oughta just leave the women and clear out. You got nothing holding you in Oakland. Me neither. We should just keep going and never come back."

"Oakland's the only place I know. It wouldn't be good for me any place else. You gotta be fine to steal as many cars as I have and get away clear. Where else am I gonna have any contacts, for the cars, the parts, the disc players?"

"We got problems, I'm tellin' you." Rudy's tone hardened. "Adenhauer knows us. He can find us if we stay around. Worse, we know him. We're a danger to him. All he needs to do is hire a couple of other dudes to take us out."

"We can't hurt him. Who's going to believe us?"

"People'll believe you. Nice, white boy. I'm the one they aren't going to believe."

Jimmy attempted a smile. "You could get a haircut. Buy a razor. Maybe a button-down shirt. Probably make a big difference."

"Hmm." Rudy's hand went to the dark stubble of his chin. "You could too. We probably should."

He turned off at North Livermore Avenue, onto First Street, drove for a few blocks, turned again, meandering through town. He finally parked under a tall shade tree behind an older car with badly worn gray paint. Jimmy stepped out of the van, walked half a block to the gas station on the corner and went into the restroom. He dumped Diane's wallet in the trash and added some more damp paper towels. He had argued with Rudy about keeping a credit card or two, but they had decided it would be better if they didn't. He returned to the van and went up to the driver's side.

Rudy rolled down the window. "Wait with the car. I'll drive the van over to the park and dump the other wallet. We'll look for a dumpster on the way out of town for the purses. Don't want anyone to see either of us carrying a purse."

"I'm smarter than that," Jimmy said.

"I'll come back by here. You can follow me the rest of the way, just in case there's any problem." He jabbed his thumb towards the rear where the women were in their sacks.

Jimmy snorted. "They're not going anywhere."

"You're right about that."

The van moved away from the curb and did a U turn in the middle of the street. Jimmy pulled out a cigarette and leaned against the car to enjoy it while he waited. In ten minutes, the van returned. Jimmy got into the car, cranked the engine twice before it started and fell in behind the other vehicle.

On the way out of town, Rudy saw the dumpster he remembered from other trips. It was to one side of the dusty parking lot next to a bait shop. He drove up to the dumpster and stopped. Jimmy parked alongside, further obscuring their activity. They kept their motors running. Rudy was in and out of the van in less than a minute. The purses were tossed in with dead night crawlers, clams and putrid garbage. There wouldn't be any dumpster divers here, Jimmy reminded himself as he rolled up his window. The stink could drop birds that flew too close.

Carol and Diane realized that they were on a freeway again, not too long this time, twenty minutes, maybe. Time was blurred. At least the blaring radio had stopped. They slowed, a stop and a turn, more curves and turns and bumps, but the stops were far apart, farther than they would be in a town. It seemed that they had been driving for hours. Sounds of other vehicles grew rare. Diane's nose cleared and she prayed it would stay that way. Then the road became very bumpy, and the going slower, a dirt road. A hint of dust penetrated the stuffy air inside the sacks. The van's tires crunched over rocks of various sizes, which flew up and hit the inside of the fenders, sounding like gun shots. Diane felt Carol jolt against her, her body tense. Over and over Diane willed her own body to relax, and hoped the message would get to Carol. Relax. Don't panic. But panic was close inside the scratchy, dark sack with her, laughing.

Diane realized she could die here. She wanted to breathe again, one long, cool breath of air before they killed her.

The van made a tight right turn and rocked to a stop. The women could hear a vehicle behind them come to a stop, too. Their driver got out and walked back to the car. A light breeze swirled some dust from the road into the open door.

The call of the Red Winged blackbird mingled with fragments of the men's talk and drifted inside. The women could not hear words, just sounds. The heat became oppressive, and

Carol started to struggle and thrash about. Even though tied in a tangled electrical cord, Diane struck back with her feet, hitting Carol solidly on her second try. Carol gave a muffled groan, but the struggling stopped.

The blackbird's song helped Diane. She tried to translate the notes, wondering whether or not they meant she should have courage and hope.

Outside, the men studied the levee and the vast acres of flat farmland that stretched below them. All was quiet. They saw no one. On the other side of the levee, visibility was not as good. At the water's edge, thick bushes, small trees, and a tangle of vines and bamboo competed for space between the high water line and the top of the levee. The water level was far higher than the level of the protected fields, but the water, too, abruptly stopped in a dense jumble of willows and blackberry vines. It was a backwater slough where fishermen might be a problem in the early morning or evening, but not likely in the middle of a hot July day. The narrow, weedy, road ran along the top of the levee and dead-ended in a tiny loop twelve feet from where the van had stopped.

"No one around." Rudy said. "Let's move them to the boat. Get 'em on their feet. I'll keep watch."

Jimmy opened the van's side door and unthreaded the extension cord binding the women's feet to the base of the seats. "Okay, sit up you two." He worked to prop up one woman, then the other.

"Ha! You don't look too good now." Jimmy said, pulling the burlap sacks from their upper bodies. He seemed surprised at how their appearance had changed. "No more rich bitch look. Red, sweaty faces, all marked up. Rumpled clothes covered with stuff." His words gained momentum. "Rat nest hair." He hoisted the women to their feet beside the van and waited for orders. Carol collapsed on the dusty roadside, her right foot asleep. Jimmy rushed to yank her on her feet and prop her next to the van. He looked at Carol, gave a slight nod toward Rudy. The fear in his face infected her.

Arms folded across his chest, Rudy continued to scan the track on the levee and fields below for any sign of activity. He seemed unconcerned that Carol had fallen and now was propped against the van trying to get the circulation back into her foot.

"Okay. Move!" said Rudy. The women moved stiffly. Carol stumbled. Rudy grabbed her arm and hustled her down the path. He ground his teeth until the group had moved down far enough not to be seen from the farmland.

In the slough a small dock braced itself against the levee. Next to the dock, overshadowing it, a derelict houseboat listed at its mooring. It was a sixty-foot, aluminum, pontoon boat with a few traces of light blue where wide stripes had once been painted.

Diane's spirits rose as her eyes squinted in the bright sunlight. The delta. That's what the blackbird was telling her. They're somewhere in the delta! Looking quickly to the right and to the left from the top of the levee, she spotted Mount Diablo and tried to note all the physical features of the area. She wasn't lost. She didn't know where she was exactly, but she wasn't lost! The slough was narrow and seemed to dead-end in both directions, but she knew that couldn't be the case. She saw the dense undergrowth along the water on the opposite levee, and beyond that, in the distance, she caught a glimpse of a large cornfield. On their side, both Carol and Diane saw the "Private Property — Keep Out" and the "Protected by Smith and Wesson" signs nailed to a post near the old dock. Diane's mind flashed to a water ski trip in 1978.

Her yell, "Hit it!" rings across flat water and bounces off the levees. The boat's bow leaps into the air with the roar of its jet engine. The brown water splits as the v-hull pushes out low bow waves and foam. Seventy-five feet back, in the center of the wake, water breaking over her head, Diane rides her slalom ski onto the surface.

There are no other boats. Early spring recess means most families have gone to the mountains for their last skiing on snow, instead of to the delta. The temperature is seventy-four, the water brisk. Her skeg rips the surface tension on her wide cuts across the wake, a delicious sound. She works hard, but soon tires and follows a leisurely pace, unwilling to give up the perfect water. She crosses wide to the left before she sees it. The snake swimming across the river holds its head high. A series of s-squiggles mark the glassy surface behind it. Neither Brad, driving, nor the observer has seen the snake. Approaching at twenty-eight miles an hour, Diane decides against any maneuver that might dump her into the water near the reptile. She catches her breath, keeps her ski stable and whooshes in front of the advancing snake. She glances back, wet hair slapping at her face. The snake, unfazed by the wakes, continues its swim.

Diane signals the boat, points at the water then back where the snake was. The observer does not understand. Brad signals he'll turn around, but Diane shakes her head and waves the boat forward.

Giving herself another quarter of a mile, she signals her intention to stop, fingers across her throat, tosses the tow line and spreads her arms wide to slow her immersion into the silty water. She hauls herself over the low freebroad with unusual speed. No one else saw the snake. Diane, Brad, the boys and the other couple continued to ski the rest of the day. No one saw any other snakes, but Diane took out the snake bite kit and reread the directions, just in case.

\*   \*   \*

The Sacramento-San Joaquin River delta composes nearly a thousand miles of waterways intertwining and joining to eventually be caught by the huge pumping stations and pulled into the State Water Project, the system that transports water to southern California through canals, pipes, reservoirs and more pumps. The water that escapes the delta pumping station eventually arrives in San Francisco Bay. The entire waterway has been in decline for years. Salt water incursion penetrating into the Central Valley along the deep water channels reverses the flushing action the rivers would bring to San Francisco Bay. The drought, the ever-increasing pressures of growing populations and years of bad water policy, all take their toll. A big fish kill was reported on a radio interview Diane heard on her drive to Danville. Had she driven to Danville just this morning? Was that the same day as this? Yet, she is heartened to realize they were somewhere in the delta.

For years, when she and Brad were first married, they had explored parts of the delta. Brad developed new computer programs for Hewlett-Packard. He worked weekends and odd hours in exchange for midweeks off. When the boys were still in diapers, they had camped on the delta in a homemade houseboat. Later, it was in the delta that the boys and their friends learned to water ski. They stopped going when Brad's job demands changed and when increased numbers of Bay Area people discovered they could launch their ski boats within an hour of their homes. The delta became too dangerous. There were too many fast boats, drunk drivers, careless skiers, serious accidents, too much noise, and too much pollution.

Yet, Diane remembered the delta trips fondly. It had been years since she had been on the water in the delta, but she felt comfortable and secure in the knowledge it was a place she knew like an old friend. One who could help her escape.

Mount Diablo is the dominant feature of the landscape, if you happen to be directly in line with it on a slough, or if you climb a levee to see it. Bridges are another point of reference, though not as helpful as the mountain.

The slough held something else. A ski boat. Right there, protected by white fenders, tied to the houseboat. It wasn't a new boat, fifteen or maybe twenty years old, she guessed. But it had been a tournament boat once. Diane knew about driving tournament boats, although jets were better if you were trying to find your way around the delta. These waters hid many submerged hazards for boat props. Her mind whirled with possibilities.

The ice cold of intense thought froze out Diane's fear. Her focus so intensified that it would have frightened her under normal stress, such as confrontations with angry constituents or employees threatening to strike. Every brain cell charged, exploded and charged again. Her eyes radiated. Indeed, her eyes might have given her away to a trained psychiatrist. In the Middle Ages, withdrawal into this kind of acute mental activity might have been called the beginning of madness.

Carol knew they were in the delta too, but she was not thrilled. She liked her water clear, not muddy. She felt imprisoned, trapped, lost. Neither woman showed much indication of her feelings, other than Diane's eyes and her very brief glances around the area when they crossed the top of the levee.

The old houseboat quivered when they stepped on board. A duck flew off excitedly, leaving behind a fresh greenish purple and white splat on the deck. Rudy unlocked the sliding glass door, pushed aside the torn curtain and motioned the women inside. "All the way back." He directed them with his gun. Jimmy followed the women inside. Rudy stayed on the front deck and watched the levee. Midway back in the boat, Carol stopped and nodded at the bathroom. Jimmy shoved her ahead.

"Yeah, well, in a minute. When we're through," Jimmy said. "This is your room, ladies. Make yourselves comfortable. Sit down."

He pushed back a filthy curtain, anchored it behind a dull green five-gallon gas can, unlocked the back door and stepped out onto the stern. Unlocking a padlock on a storage box, he pulled out some nylon ski rope and what looked like old clothesline. He relocked the box, stepped inside, and left the door open with a shred of the curtain hooked on the handle.

"I'm just airing the place out. Don't get any ideas. None at all, you hear?" He tossed the lines on the floor.

Two sets of frightened eyes looked up at him from the bunks. In unison they looked from him to the door and back again. "Understand?" he asked again, louder. The women nodded that they understood. He went forward, took two beers from a cooler already on board, popped one open and joined Rudy on the front deck, closing the door.

"They could be our mothers, you know." Jimmy kept his voice low. He'd seen the pictures in their wallets. The one named Diane Lind had several pictures. There was one of her with her husband when they were about fifteen years younger and pictures of her boys, taken together when they were toddlers, high school and college graduation pictures, and finally, one son and his wife. Carol Steadhold, too, kept family pictures in her wallet, although not as many. She had two sons also and lots of membership cards for different organizations.

"We need more ice. Beer's barely cold," said Rudy.

# Chapter 10

Plainly worried about the short, poorly written brief he had finished reading, Roger Steadhold phoned back to Canby headquarters on an in-flight telephone. He was informed that Evert Johns was in Washington, so he asked for his own secretary. When Phyllis answered, he skipped the usual pleasantries. "This brief is worse than useless. Who prepared it? I mean who dictated it? I'm landing in New York with nothing to take into the 'emergency meeting.' Is there anything you know about why I was ordered out on such short notice? I can't reach Evert or his secretary."

"Janet is right here. I'll put her on."

Evert Johns, Canby International's president and CEO, stood six feet five inches tall. To shake hands with the man gave one an immediate sense of his great physical strength, and of his character. He did not have the overly gregarious manner of some CEOs, nor the fiercely predatory drive that motivated others. He was a quiet man whom some people considered a cold, insensitive elitist. In truth, he had genuine affection for his intellectual equals. Ideas fascinated him. He would probe and test them, occasionally arguing one side, then another, and another. He recognized good ideas when he heard them, and he was one of those rare individuals who could appreciate and use constructive criticism. Roger was among those who had earned Evert Johns highest regard, so were most of the executive secretaries.

"Mr. Johns is in Washington, DC. He flew out Monday evening," said Janet. "He knows your schedule. I mentioned it to him when he called this morning. Normally, he doesn't copy me when he e-mails people, and I haven't seen the report you're talking about."

Roger noticed that she volunteered nothing more. He waited, but she waited too. There would be nothing more. The message, if there was one, was in her words and the measured way in which they had been spoken. He knew she could have said more, could have speculated, but she was keeping herself in check.

The silence on the line became ponderous. He gave up. "Okay, thanks very much. If there's anything else, you have my itinerary."

"Watch out for muggers, Roger."

"I will. Please ask my office to call Carol and let her know that I've no idea when I'll get back to California. Catch you later."

He hung up the phone, wondering what the hell was going on.

At the houseboat, a half-hour passed. Carol began making sounds as loud as she could with the tape over her mouth.

Rudy went in and ripped the duct tape off her mouth. She looked like she was wearing bright pink war paint in a wide stripe across the bottom of her face.

"What is it, bitch?"

"I need to go to the bathroom," she said.

"Jimmy, you want to take care of this?" he said, stomping up front again. "I didn't bargain for any of this."

Angry and disgusted, he seemed to be trying to block the whole scene out of his mind. He went onto the front deck and stared at the sky, shaking his head.

Jimmy went back with a kitchen knife and sawed through the flexcuff binding Carol's wrists. "No tricks."

Carol disappeared into the tiny bathroom and closed her eyes when she closed the door. The stench was terrible. She opened her eyes, but she almost couldn't pee because of the stink in the place. No toilet paper, no soap.

"I suppose you've got to go, too?"

Jimmy looked at Diane. She nodded. He started to peel the duct tape off her mouth as gently as he could, but her eyes squeezed shut and tears rolled down her face. She squeaked with each tug.

Rudy returned. "We could leave the tape on this one, but it's fun to rip it off. Move. Let me do it."

It took two good, hard tugs to rip the tape away. Each caused an involuntary cry from Diane. She, too, had a stripe across the bottom of her face, but hers was red, sprouting little spots of blood on the right side and on her right upper lip where some skin had come off. She stared, wild-eyed at the open sliding glass door.

"Can you close the door so snakes won't come in? I'm afraid."

"Snakes. How stupid! What snake can get on a houseboat?"

"They can crawl on the dock the same way we came."

"No snakes are going to come on this boat! I don't know why I'm standing here talking to this bitch." Rudy stomped forward again. "Leave it open, Jimmy. We need the air. If some critter comes in, the old bags can keep it company."

Carol came out of the bathroom. Rudy turned to keep her in sight and noticed her wedding rings. He charged at her and grabbed at her left hand. She pulled away.

"Give 'em to me."

Carol didn't protest. Getting the engagement ring and the companion wedding band off was difficult. Her fingers had swollen in the heat, and her nervous tugging at them didn't help.

"I can cut the fingers off," Rudy said, smiling. "We might want a little something to send to your husband."

Finally she twisted the rings free and handed them to him.

"Tie this one up, Jimmy."

Jimmy used the nylon line to secure her hands to the bunk post. He was rough and sloppy, tying her hands together in front of her.

With the self-confidence of one used to intimidating people, Rudy put his pistol in his belt, pulled out his butterfly knife and cut Diane's hands free. After giving up her wedding rings, she was permitted to use the bathroom.

"Tie that one up when she comes out," he ordered and went forward to examine the new loot.

When she finished in the bathroom, Jimmy used the old clothesline to tie Diane's hands to the end of the other bunk. She could see the stern of the ski boat through the open sliding glass door. Carol squirmed. It was hot. Forward, Rudy paced back and forth, becoming increasingly agitated. He returned to the bunkroom as Jimmy finished tying Diane's hands.

"We're going to have a party tonight, old girls," he said to Carol and grabbed her hair, jerking her head backwards. "A real good time." Rudy ran his other hand up her thigh.

"Don't — " Carol started to struggle, but Rudy beat her head against the metal post.

"Hey, bitch. You'll like it. I promise you."

"Raping grandmothers will do a whole lot for your image," Diane said.

Her cold voice infuriated him. Still facing Carol, Rudy's expression stormed with red and purple anger, his facial muscles twitching. He erupted, suddenly striking Diane across the face with the back of his hand as he swung around. Then he hit her again, the flat of his hand swinging back the other way. Dark red blood ran from her nose. Bright welts showed at once on both sides of her face. Blood, beginning to coagulate on her upper lip where the skin had been pulled away, flowed anew. Her right eye began to swell.

Jimmy's hands began moving up and down from his face, then to the back of his head. "Let's go, Rudy. It's time to go. We need to ditch the van. Come on, Rudy. Let's go."

Finally, Rudy followed Jimmy to the bow. Incoherent sounds of a brief, agitated conversation drifted back to the women, then Rudy left the houseboat. He paused at the top of the levee and looked down the road. He took two more steps through tall, dry grass toward the driver's side of the van before he heard a rattling sound. He leaped backward. As he backed further away, the rattling sound stopped. Rudy squared his shoulders, drew a deep breath, turned and let himself in the passenger side.

Carol and Diane heard the van start, and the tires spit gravel as it sped away. On the bow, Jimmy opened the cooler and fished out the last beer, wiped it on his jeans and popped it open.

Diane bent her head over to her shackled hands and pinched her nose closed to try to stop the bleeding. Pain pounded through her eyes and made her dizzy. She then tried tilting her head back and gagged. It felt like she was swallowing a quart of her own blood, but staying calm and holding her head back seemed to help.

By the time Jimmy came back to the bunkroom the blood had dried in dark crimson crusts and smears along the courseways over her face. Jimmy's angular face reflected in the dirty glass when he pulled the outside door shut, latched it and drew the dusty rag of a curtain across. The reflection reminded Diane of a primitive hunter transplanted from northern Europe, beyond any civilization, thousands of years ago. I must fit right in, she thought, a swollen, bloody Neanderthal.

Jimmy turned. "No noise. Not a sound or you're dead. You don't want to upset my friend. He's not predictable."

Jimmy lied to the women, telling them Rudy would be back at any moment. In fact, Rudy had taken the van back to Livermore, a big risk considering it was probably reported stolen by now. Rudy apparently didn't trust Jimmy to do the job, so Jimmy was left to guard the women until four. At four, he was to take the car and drive to Livermore and meet Rudy at a pizza place. Jimmy wasn't sure of the plan past that point, but it was time for him to get going.

He double-checked to be sure the small windows were secured and covered. He then closed the passageway door and went forward. The women heard the latch click and the sliding glass door slam shut, and then they felt the slight motion of the boat as he stepped onto the dock.

Diane and Carol instantly started to whisper and struggle with the ropes tying their hands. The temperature in the closed bunkroom began to rise.

"Oh, Diane, I'm so sorry, but thanks for distracting him."

"We're in for much worse ..." Diane coughed and spit blood on the floor. When she could continue, she said, "I have a plan, Carol. Unless you have any ideas?"

"What is it?"

"This slough dead ends that way."

She nodded her head to the stern.

"It's choked with water hyacinths. Not a single boat has come by since we've been here."

Carol stopped pulling at her rope and waited for the plan. The rotted old clothes line around Diane's wrists released a small cloud of fibers and dust when she rubbed it vigorously up and down the metal post of the bunk, but after that initial promise, it held firm. Carol went back to working on her nylon bonds with her teeth, attempting to undo the knots. They both became calmer. Frenzied activity wasn't helping. Diane slowly pulled the line up and down the entire length of the hollow, metal post. It was square shaped and near the top, the rope snagged, and snagged again. She worked the rope back and forth hoping to snag it deliberately, and pull away one fiber at a time, but the line now passed smoothly over the rough spot. She needed to try something else.

"When we get free, I'll check the ski boat and see if I can find the keys. You search in here, in the drawers, cupboards, everywhere. If you find some keys, or you hear the boat start, come running. We'll need water, any food you can find and plastic bags. If there's a map of the delta, grab it too."

"Okay."

"Also, if you have a chance to escape, take it, with or without me. The important thing is for at least one of us to get away. Agreed?"

"Yeah," Carol said. "Same for you."

"If the boat keys are around here, they're probably some place out of sight but still convenient," Diane said. "The boat's our best hope, but if we can't use it, we go into the water. Upstream, toward the hyacinths, and across. There's a lot of cover, undergrowth and some trees. Head over there with any of the stuff you can collect. Hide right in the thickest part."

"Why not use the road? Get as far away as we can?"

"It's just what they'll expect us to do. The countryside's too open, you can see for miles, and it's on someone's private property. The only car coming along is likely to be those two who kidnapped us. We'd be going out the same way they'll be coming back. The field below us is in tomatoes. No place to hide. We could go into the water if we can't use the boat, but we can't move fast in the water and they have the guns and the key to the ski boat.

"No matter what, if you hear a car, go over the side and try to get to that other levee. Hide under this thing, if they surprise us."

"This? The houseboat?"

"There's all kinds of space between the pontoons and probably a matting of decaying cattails and whatever other vegetation has drifted in and stuck. This houseboat hasn't been moved in years."

Diane kept working on the knot while she talked. By leaning forward and shifting her position slightly she could loosen the pressure on it. It didn't slip easily the way the nylon line would have, but Carol was having no more luck than she was. Then Diane saw it, the line that had to be pushed through to release the knot. At first, her squirming had tightened the knot, but she was more determined and patient now. She tugged at the line with her teeth, stopped to inspect, tugged some more and stopped to inspect again.

Still studying the knot she said, "If we can't use the ski boat, I'll need your shoes."

Carol kicked them off without a word. She started pulling harder on one of the cords with her teeth, the way Diane was doing.

"If we don't find the keys, and you've collected what you can, leave. Don't wait for me. If they see me, I'm caught. If I'm lucky and can make them angry, they'll shoot me before they think to torture me to find you. This has got to be the stupidest kidnapping —. How can they possibly use either of us? We're nothing to them."

"They wanted Roger, remember? Cripes, my head aches," Carol said.

"Oh, yeah. Okay, I get it. They can use you. Not me," Diane said.

Diane tugged at the knot again with her teeth. Millimeter by millimeter the knot was loosening. When it relaxed, she almost ruined everything with a sudden motion that threatened to tighten it again. She paused and took three deep breaths. Where was the end of the rope? There it was. She pulled the loop through and her hands were free. Leaping over to Carol and pushing the nylon line back into its own knots, Diane quickly untied the ski line that bound Carol. "Let's go."

She unlocked the door and was outside and into the ski boat without another word. Carol went in the other direction looking for things they might use and for the keys. Diane's nose started bleeding again, leaving a trail of red dots and smudges. She tried pinching her nose tightly, but she was moving too much and needed both hands to search for the keys so she ignored it, except to wipe at it with the back of her hand.

Checking all the compartments, everywhere, she found an oily rag under the observer seat and some moldy life vests, a bottle opener, and an empty beer can. She ran her hands up under the side along the steering cables — nothing. She even lifted the engine cover, again nothing. A thought struck her. Since Carol hadn't found the keys yet, she probably wouldn't. Diane pushed the engine cover all the way back, grabbed the rag and, using the sharp end of the bottle opener, jabbed as much cloth as she could into the small vent at the back of the cover. Taking too much time, she thought, while she pursued her scorched earth policy, pushing to cut off the engine's ventilation. She could hear cupboards opening, closing, as Carol searched inside the houseboat. Diane stepped back aboard the houseboat and grabbed the dull green gas can by the sliding door. It lifted too easily, but something sloshed in the bottom so she hauled it into the ski boat. Unscrewing the top, she poured what she guessed to be a gallon, plus or minus, into the bilge under the engine. She stuffed the moldy life preservers into the engine compartment and, replacing the engine cover, she took another valuable minute to lean over the driver's seat and pump the hand throttle vigorously. The trap might or might not work. No more time on this.

Carol appeared at the stern. "No keys. Plan B."

"Yeah."

Smears of blood were all over the place, everything she had touched. She handed the gas can over to Carol who accepted it without question. "Just put it there," Diane said and scampered back into the houseboat and picked up Carol's high heels along with her own.

"Any plastic bags?"

Carol held up two grocery bags and a large, thicker garbage bag. She had dumped the contents on the floor.

"It looks like fairly clean garbage," Carol said. Beer cans, empty chip packages, fast food containers lay in a pile on the floor.

"Strip to your underwear and put your clothes in one that's air tight. Leave a smaller one for me. Any food or water, anything to drink?"

"Not much."

"Take it and get out of here as fast as you can. If I see them coming, I'll yell to high heaven. Drop everything and go."

Diane, still leaving a trail of droplets, headed for the bow. The handle of the sliding glass door slipped from her grasp at her first attempt to open the door. She had forgotten to unlock it. She rushed onto the dock and up the levee, paused briefly to survey the road and surroundings. It looked very much like they were on a dead end slough. The road behind her was a dead end, for sure. She bundled the shoes next to her chest. Running as hard as she could in her stocking feet, Diane headed up the open end of the road for a little over a hundred yards. There she stopped, brought one of her shoes up to her battered face and wiped her nose on it, then coughed up some more blood and spit it on the shoe. She threw it as far as she could up the road ahead of her. It landed squarely in the middle. No one could miss it unless they came at night.

Next, she dropped one of Carol's shoes on the edge of the road in the dead grass, not at all obvious. Turning back and taking care to run along the edge where there was some vegetation to cushion her feet, Diane dropped her other shoe in easy sight. Racing now, she crossed the levee, and started down to the houseboat. She turned one last time, squatted down and studied the road, poking her head just enough above the line of vegetation to see, but not so high as to be seen. She looked out across what seemed to be miles of open country and saw nothing unusual but the shoe in the middle of the road, then the one by the side of the road.

She retreated quickly, leaving Carol's last shoe with its heel stuck in the planking of the old dock. Her linen jacket was off and she was undoing her skirt as she stepped into the houseboat. Carol was gone. Diane stuffed her skirt and jacket into a Safeway bag, unbuttoned her blouse, shed it along with her half-slip and the tight little roll of her pantyhose, pulled off inside out. Diane pushed the rest of the clothes into the bag and tied the handles into a knot while stepping into the ski boat. From the platform at the stern, she eased herself into the still, brown water, so filled with silt that anything disappeared from sight an inch below the surface. A line of small bubbles betrayed where Carol had crossed. Maybe the wind would come up and disperse them.

The plastic bag had some air trapped in it. The water was surprisingly deep off the end of the boat. Diane couldn't touch bottom with her head above the surface. She wondered if it might be high tide but didn't stop to be sure. Hide first, then worry about the little stuff. She sidestroked across, jerking the barely floating grocery bag along with her. Her foot touched soft, sucking mud and she stood in a low crouch to avoid the overhanging vegetation and struggled to wade into the brush, believing the muck would hold her eventually, even as her feet sank to the ankles. The water was warm, but not as hot as her body had been. She wanted to stay in it longer but dared not. She tried to wipe her face. It hurt. Even water stung it.

"Diane, over here," came a hushed whisper.

"I didn't see you. Except for the bubbles, I wouldn't have known you were here."

"Diane, tell me something. You're not really afraid of snakes, are you?" Carol asked, helping Diane onto the bank under the branches.

"I don't like to be surprised by them, but I know that if I leave them alone they'll leave me alone."

"Well, for the record, I am."

Diane managed a half smile. The flow of blood had slowed to little trickles mixed with delta water. Her face hurt, but the water had washed away some of the caked blood. With her good eye she studied the shoreline undergrowth, deciding it was at the high water mark and maybe in the slack period. With a dead end, she wasn't sure of the effect. Some places in the delta the tidal high and low extremes could vary up to eight feet. This arm seemed unusually deep for a dead end.

The women concentrated on making themselves invisible. The two white plastic bags with their clothes went into the larger black one. The thick undergrowth snagged and scratched their skin. Fortunately, there were plenty of dead cattails, soft and spongy. The day was very hot. Stunted willows and other trees provided shade. Jumbled roots clung desperately to the levee, while the water, which would eventually win the trees away from the bank, sucked at the branches that bounced and played on the surface when Carol or Diane moved.

"Diane, I should tell you something. In the houseboat while I was searching though the drawers. I found a color photo of Roger and me and the Nettles. Roger's head was circled. It was the day of the stockholders meeting, at the end of June."

"A photo? Of you?"

"Uh huh, we were headed into the Canby building when we noticed a man, some street person, I thought at the time. He took a couple of flash pictures. It was weird, but we were preoccupied and rushed. This whole thing must be some kind of attempt to get Roger. They must have wanted to kidnap or kill him. Remember? At the house, they asked where he was. Thank God, he's in New York."

"No wonder they were less than thrilled when we showed up. It's not a complete mistake, though. They can use you to get at him."

"Anyhow, I hid the photo behind the drawer. I thought it could possibly prove a connection with these men. Or help us some way, later, if we live through this."

Carol's words made sense, but she squeaked oddly when a large stinkbug charged over her left knee and headed up her thigh. In the commotion to escape the beetle, she put her face through a cobweb whose owner jumped on her upper arm and at once began marching closer to her face.

"Or, even if we don't live through it," Diane said, flicking the big, yellow and black garden spider off Carol, who trembled and mewed like a distressed cat.

Diane said, "I'm feeling much better now that we're here and not over there in that boat,"

Yet, seeing her friend's grave unease, Diane realized that Carol was probably more frightened and uncomfortable hidden in the bushes than she had been on the houseboat tied to a bunk.

Lots of people hated the delta, the insects, the mud, the silty water, the occasional dead animal, not to mention the real biological and chemical hazards. Diane hoped to control her friend's near panic by encouraging her to concentrate on the other things instead of the bugs.

"Wonder how they're doing in Sacramento without us. I sure hope they miss us enough to call around."

The meeting of California Elected Women was to start at noon in the County Supervisors' building. Carol was expected early to confer beforehand with the director. "I mean, I know they'll do fine without us," Diane said, "but Brad is in Japan for another three weeks. The only way I'll be missed is when I don't show up for all the meetings I have."

"Roger left for New York this morning. He didn't know for how long." Carol, continuing to tremble, became somber and thoughtful. "Several days at least. No one's going to really miss us. Not enough to search for us! Even if they miss us, no one would know where to look. We're lost. We don't even know where we are."

"Easy, Carol. We're not that lost. We're not lost at all. I just might not take the shortest way out of here, that's all, but we're not lost. Okay? Pretend you're on a camping trip." Carol winced at the suggestion.

"I know you've been camping," Diane said quickly, not wanting any argument. "You can get a nice hot shower when you get home. In the meantime, just relax and try to ignore the unpleasantness." She had hoped to make it sound better than her words conveyed.

"You want me to make friends with the dirt and the bugs?"

Carol punctuated her sentence by viciously slapping a large red ant on her arm. But her fear was infectious. Although Diane could handle most of the inconveniences of the delta, she knew their captors meant to kill them. She knew. She sensed the dispassionate cruelty, especially in the one who had threatened them. The worry could begin playing tricks with her mind.

\*   \*   \*

In Sacramento, CEW's director, Evelyn Day, had called the office on the Cal State campus, and asked the intern to call Carol and Diane's homes and offices. They were overdue. She knew that they had planned to drive together because she had talked to Carol the previous day. The other executive board members were coming from all over the state. Two women legislators were going to be there, supervisors, council members and school trustees, along with the Kern County Coroner and San Francisco's City Attorney. Worried, Evelyn also instructed the intern to call the Highway Patrol to check on accidents.

The meeting began on time with Evelyn explaining her concern and the hope that they would arrive shortly. The Finance Director, a council member from West Hollywood, ran the meeting when the legislator who was vice president had to leave early. Considering the situation, the meeting progressed as well as it could. The critical business was completed. No one was angry, merely concerned. These were busy women, motivated by their interest in mentoring more women into the political process.

Evelyn Day was scheduled to take two vacation days beginning Thursday, but promised to keep trying to track down her missing president and treasurer. The intern called during the meeting to say the highway patrol had nothing to report.

Carol and Diane organized as best they could, hanging one or two pieces of clothing at a time on the branches to dry. One bag had not been completely waterproof. A breeze rippled the water. The hot, dry air, even with all the water around, quickly dried their things. The food inventory discouraged Diane when she learned all that Carol collected was a diet cola, a half empty bottle of aspirin and a rusty can of Spam.

"What about that box of crackers on the counter?" Diane asked.

"Don't ask. Cockroaches were playing in it. Not many crackers, anyway. There were a few loose jellybeans melted in the bottom drawer, but there were more bugs there too. I left 'em."

"I think I'll skip lunch and wait for dinner."

Returning from the California Elected Women's meeting, Louise Renne, City Attorney of San Francisco, was fiddling with her car phone, keeping one eye on the road as she headed back to the city. She worried about Carol and Diane. She used her car phone only when absolutely necessary. Something was wrong. Diane and she were due to be on a panel together at a conference of women architects in the city in a few days. They had planned to discuss their presentation on the appointments process, and why and how more qualified women could serve on state boards and commissions.

Louise crossed the Richmond-San Rafael Bridge and drove through Marin County at her usual speed, even though she knew there was nothing she could do to avoid going across the Golden Gate Bridge and into San Francisco with the five o'clock traffic. It did move better going into San Francisco than out, but only a little. Eventually, she parked in her designated spot at City Hall, went through the metal detector, greeted the guard by name and continued up to her office on the second floor.

The building, like the Opera House that was once magnificent enough to host the authors of the United Nations charter, was in disrepair. The damage from the 1989 Loma Prieta earthquake had been the final insult. Reinforcement beams and temporary structures braced the walls supporting the rotunda. Scaffolding filtered its beauty. Warning signs were posted everywhere, reminding people that they were there at their own risk, not that that would mean much in case someone were seriously injured and decided to sue, the City Attorney reminded herself.

Three staff attorneys waited to see her. Walking into her inner office with the first attorney, Louise asked her secretary to call Diane Lind and Mayor Carol Steadhold's homes. If there was no response, she was to call the Highway Patrol state headquarters in Sacramento and inquire, officially, about any accident that morning. She gave the details hurriedly. Inside her office, the city's top legal officer put her briefcase down on one end of the oval conference table, offered the young attorney a soda or a bottled water, twisted the cap off a water for herself, poured it into a glass then gave him her full attention.

He seemed harried and nervous about his strategy with some new developments in the case that would be in court in the morning. Just being in her office apparently had a calming affect upon him, however. He winked at a whimsical, papier-mâché woman, reclining along the counter that topped the lower shelves. The robust figure in a polka dot dress had her eyes closed and a smile on her lips. Louise, in her familiar surroundings, inhaled deeply.

On low, dark wood shelving and on part of the wall just under the windows, were the best of the hard hat and baseball cap collection she had acquired over the years. Also under the tall windows was a comfortable, inviting sofa with a long coffee table in front of it, the table's only adornment, a large, burnished metal, Asian bowl. The soft, rich carpet in a deep shade of Blackcap raspberry simultaneously soothed and invigorated visitors. There was no desk. Law books lined two walls, floor to the ceiling. The graceful, large windows faced Civic Center Park, the green open space that covered a multi-storied underground parking garage for the area. The park was a place where the homeless congregated, underscoring the complex social issues of the dynamic city where, like its city hall, grandeur and ruin embraced.

The staff attorney and his boss sat in two of the six comfortable, leather chairs at the Queen Anne conference table. She listened intently. She knew the case, immediately grasped the complexity of the new complications, and understood the attorney's, and therefore the city's, anxiety. After some discussion the staff attorney rose to leave.

93

"Thank you for seeing me. It helps. You're such a nice lady."

"I'll take that as a compliment," Louise said, alerting him not to use the phrase again.

The other two attorneys came in together. Their progress report on an investigation was due, and they wanted to brief their boss before the mayor's news conference in the morning.

Heading home after seven, she was concerned that there still was no news of Diane and Carol. All in all, it had been a good day. She would locate her friends in the morning.

# Chapter 11

In Livermore, Rudy ditched the stolen van in the movie theater lot, found a barbershop, and ordered a hair cut and a shave. Why not? He had a little extra cash. The barber seemed quite pleased at his results, and showed the customer his reflection in the mirror, but Rudy made no response. He mumbled an empty thanks, paid the price without tipping and stalked out of the shop. The barber shook his head and set about decontaminating his scissors.

From the barber's, Rudy went to the western store on First Street and bought a shirt, probably thinking it helped him blend with Livermore and the valley. He left his black T-shirt on the dressing room floor. The new shirt was the most ordinary, dweeby one he could find. He hated western shirts. He checked his watch and hiked to the pizza place where he ordered a large sausage and pepperoni pizza. He knew he would have to share it when Jimmy showed up before the pizza was ready. Jimmy's expression of surprise said all Rudy needed to know about his new appearance. They split a pitcher of beer while they ate and talked quietly in a corner.

"Adenhauer is going to worry if he doesn't hear from us soon. I better call him when we finish," Rudy said. "At least we got the Steadhold dame. He'll be pissed about the other one, but we don't have to mention her. Let him find her. We have a little time. Besides, that powerboat is mine. It's registered to me. I paid cash for it."

"Yeah, but it was Adenhauer's cash," Jimmy said, trying to stall. He did not want to return to the houseboat. Rudy would want to shoot the other woman, or worse, make him kill her. But Rudy seemed to have changed more than his appearance.

"The boat's mine. If I can't use it, at least I can resell it. It's legally mine. I've got the papers." Rudy's voice rose menacingly.

"Okay. Okay. Want to see a movie while we wait."

"Can't do nothin' tonight." Rudy was trying to think. "Don't want Adenhauer to come sneaking around and catch us with our pants down." Rudy gave a short, bark of a laugh.

"Want another pitcher?" Jimmy asked.

"No. And I don't think we should drive back to houseboat tonight. I ain't sleepin' on that hot, shitty, stinkin' houseboat, neither. Let's get a room in town, see what Adenhauer says. We can go out early in the morning."

They stopped at an old motel on the edge of town. "Gimme a room with *two* beds," Rudy said. "And a working TV. We want the business rate."

The woman frowned, looked out the window at the beat-up car. In a flat voice, she said, "Certainly, sir. All I need is your business card."

Rudy, in no mood to be denied, replied, "I used my last one today, but my associate has some. Just a minute."

Jimmy was leaning against the car having a smoke when Rudy yelled to him.

"Need one of your business cards, Jimmy."

"Sure thing."

He fumbled with his wallet and produced several frayed cards which read, "Thrasher Auto Parts, New and Used, Jimmy Thrasher, Principal," and a telephone number. The address was a post office box in Oakland. He separated one from the others with a dirty fingernail and handed it to Rudy who delivered it to the woman behind the counter.

In the privacy of the room, the two men planned to figure out what to say to Adenhauer. They turned on the sports channel, flopped back lazily on their beds and fell asleep, missing the appointed time to call. When Rudy did call, he got an answering machine.

"Hey, Mr. Adenhauer. We got your order. Had to make the substitution we talked about, but she's all tied up for you. A surprise package, like. Where in the hell are you, anyway? I'll call again at midnight."

From the motel they drove to Oakland, stopped by Jimmy's one-room apartment, then Rudy's. They loaded some of their personal belongings into the car, in case Adenhauer got too upset. They stopped for burgers and bought a couple of six packs to bring back to the room in Livermore for a late snack. Jimmy noticed that Rudy was becoming irritable. He knew Rudy would probably kill the women, at least the extra one, no matter what he said. He dreaded returning to the houseboat. Watching Rudy pace back and forth in the tiny motel room made him nervous. Rudy had decided he liked boating, for some reason. He kept talking about it.

"We'll get the ski boat first thing in the morning and take it to that consignment place in Stockton."

"We don't have a trailer."

"I know that, dipshit! One of us will go by water and the other one can drive the car. I can go the same way we brought it in."

"Adenhauer met us at the dock and showed us the way that time," Jimmy said.

Jimmy wasn't at all sure Rudy knew how to get to Stockton by water, even if they had a map of the waterway, which they didn't. He tried a new subject.

"We can talk to Adenhauer, see how he reacts, go get the boat and —"

Rudy cut him off. "If we don't make contact with the man tonight, I'm thinkin' we should take the boat and leave. Period."

97

"Hey, wait. He wants the Steadhold woman, and he owes us money. He might need us for something else, later. Who knows?"

"The man isn't going to pay us. I've worked it out, Jimmy. He could be shittin' us. Think about it. We can identify him, even if we don't have the right name."

Still hiding in the undergrowth and thick willows toward the dead end of the slough, the two women were exhausted physically and emotionally. Diane explained that the country was too open and isolated. It would be safer to move after dark, so during the afternoon, they had permitted themselves to sleep. Diane knew it was a psychological escape. She had always caught up on her sleep during final exams in college, and she convinced herself it was a good idea. She convinced Carol by telling her about her plan to move across the cornfield in the twilight and about how the mosquitoes would be much worse at dusk and during the night. There were none now, but Diane knew they'd be fierce later, especially where they were. She concentrated on the trivial in an effort to keep them both calm. It worked. They both dozed.

Almost imperceptibly, the late afternoon breeze picked up. It ruffled the water's surface and gave a gentle, soothing motion to the foliage enfolding the sleepers. A Great Blue Heron flew back to her favorite evening haunt earlier than usual. The huge wings flapped quietly as she landed on a sturdy limb overhanging the water. The bird stayed on the limb for half an hour, scarcely moving, eyes glazed except when there was a motion or shadow that was out of the ordinary, then its eyes intensified. Sometimes the bird extended its neck ever so slowly in one direction or another. When a hapless minnow came too close to the surface, the bird had it in her beak so quickly that the little fish seemed to have jumped there all by itself. The heron, with its prey secure, took her time eating. She shook her head and tossed the fish around so that it would slide down her throat, head first. Several stretching motions conveyed it down the inside of the long neck.

The bird moved from the limb and began stalking among the undergrowth. Carol slept with her face exposed to the play of light and shadow of the leafy canopy. Diane had fallen into a fitful sleep almost at once, but woke within forty minutes. Her face was badly swollen and turning dark blue around the eyes. She rested and dozed lightly with her right arm crooked over her forehead, partially covering her eyes. She caught the motion of the heron when it moved from the tree and started its slow hunt toward her. Thrilled to see the magnificent bird at such close range, Diane kept as motionless as she could and still breathe. Sometimes, her view was completely obstructed by the undergrowth, but now and then she could see the bird. The heron had striking black wing and head markings. Salmon pink speckled the whitish bib that extended from the neck to the breast and to the ridge on the leading edge of the wings. The heron, this close, presented a spectacle far more exotic than the soft blue-gray impression one had from viewing these creatures from a distance. The elegant head faced toward the water's edge, extended slowly, then froze in position, eyes alert. In the matted, dense undergrowth there were slight movements, motions inconsistent with the effect of the breeze on the bushes or the water.

Roused by the pressure of the heron's steps, a small garter snake had no chance. The heron struck like a flash of a laser, pulling her head back with the snake lashing wildly from both sides of the strong beak that broke its spine in two places.

Carol groaned and awoke to see the heron swing around and glare at her with fierce, hard, yellow eyes, a snake writhing about the beak that held it fast. Carol squeezed her eyes shut. It was so close to her, she felt her chest would collapse. She couldn't breathe. Her heartbeat threatened to break her eardrums. The palms of her hands ran wet with sweat. Somewhere, just beyond this slough, there was other activity on the water.

In the lingering July dusk, a bass boat moved along the quiet backwaters, the driver guiding the silent, tiny electric motor with his foot. Two teen-agers cast expertly towards the shore on either side of the slough, wherever the weeds and cover were right for bass. They did not talk. Slowly, they glided up the slough, approaching the houseboat. The stillness exploded with sound and motion.

"AAAARRRKK! AAAAKKKKKKK!"

The Pterodactyl call of the Great Blue Heron rang out, startling the fishermen. The huge bird flapped her wings trying to gain altitude quickly as it burst from the undergrowth.

"AAAARRRKKKK!" came the primitive call again.

At first the bird headed upstream to follow the water route out of the slough, but she veered suddenly and headed over the levee toward the fields when she saw the fishing boat.

"Yow!" The young fisherman with his foot guiding the motor made a U-turn. "That's it for this slough."

"No matter how often that happens, they always surprise me. Right out of the Age of Dinosaurs." Within forty-five seconds, the boys stowed their gear, lowered the heavy motor and roared away.

The teenagers assumed that they had frightened the heron, but only when she broke cover had the huge bird noticed their boat. Something much closer had interrupted her tranquil meal.

Carol's movements and sounds were too much for the heron. She turned toward the water, lunged forward through the entangling branches, unfolded her great wings with some commotion and flew out over the water, dropping the snake over the hyacinths and screaming with fury.

Carol, her eyes still shut tightly, brought her hands to her face, trying to escape the vision of the yellow eyed bird with the snake.

"It's okay." Diane shook her arm gently.

The women were completely unaware of the teenagers close by who could have rescued them, until they heard the large motor fire to life a minute later.

Diane sat up and saw the snake's death dance over the bed of hyacinths. While she watched, she noticed something else: certain plants rising and falling, something under the surface

100

moving rapidly towards the struggling snake. Before the thought completely formed, the hog bass struck, crashing up through the surface, mouth agape, taking in the whole flailing snake before falling back to the surface, plants and spray flying in a huge splash. Large Mouth, Diane thought to herself. Carol groaned again.

"It's gone," Diane said. "It flew away." They had more water to cross. No need to have Carol worry about the creatures living in it.

"Oh, God. Did you see that ugly thing with the snake wiggling in its mouth?"

"She was beautiful, but it was a little scary seeing her practically on top of us."

"She? Beautiful?"

"It was a Great Blue Heron. The males have two long feathers that extend from the back of the head," Diane said. "This one was a female."

"Oh, who cares? I hate this place."

Somewhere, beyond their range of sight, came the sound of a boat. Both women concentrated on the sound of the bass boat's big motor. It was closer than any other human sound they had heard since their escape, but not close enough and it was moving away. Both women thought about the kidnappers. With little effort, they could see the houseboat and the old ski boat. Nothing had changed. The boat they heard was beyond the levee. Neither spoke. The thought that they'd missed being rescued was too depressing.

In Cupertino an answering machine clicked on.

"Hi, Diane. This is Helen in the superintendent's office. We need to know if you're going to the reception at Santa Clara University tomorrow. It's for the educational leaders who helped with the board member training sessions this past year. I have to let them know. The superintendent's going. I thought you said you could, too. Please give me a call."

A second message soon followed the previous one.

"Hi Mom. It's Brandon. Is it okay if I have some friends up to the lake this weekend? The water skiing should be great. It'll be the usual group, so there will be someone we trust to drive the boat besides me. Everyone's checked out on the house rules. Oh, you're invited too, Mom, if you want to come. Talk to you soon."

In a message from the CEW office at Sac State, the caller reminded Diane of the meeting and wondered aloud where she was.

A message later in the afternoon was a reminder about tennis on Thursday, and then another message from CEW, Evelyn Day, the director, calling this time. An early evening call from Louise Rene's office asked Diane to call back when she could.

# Chapter 12

Checking into his New York hotel, Roger found a message waiting for him from Evert Johns. It requested that he call as soon as he arrived. The hotel clerk had added two exclamation points after the word *urgent*. Roger put in a call to Carol first. The machine answered. He was disappointed but not surprised that she wasn't home.

"Hi, hon. I arrived safely. I'm here at the Biltmore. The office will be able to track me down if you need to reach me. They have all the meeting times and places, and will be able to get right through. Once I have some idea of how long I have to be here, I'll call you. I'll try to reach you tomorrow night either way. Love you, Darling, bye."

It took about four minutes to reach Evert Johns, who had left word to put through Roger's call on a top priority basis.

"Roger?"

"Yeah, I just got in."

"Can you get out to La Guardia and meet me tonight? We can grab a bite to eat at the airport. I'll need to fly back here to Washington after we meet. Things have been hectic, but I did get your message. I agree that we need to talk, face-to-face, but it has to be brief. I've commitments I can't cancel."

"I agree. I can be there. I'll catch a cab right away. What flight?"

"I'm using the company jet. Can't get into National when I return so we'll park it at Dulles. Maybe we can get this all cleared up, and you can fly home with me Friday night. What the hell you doing in New York anyway?"

"Damned if I know. I got an e-mail from you — or did I?"

"I didn't send any e-mail to you. Not lately. Keep a lid on all this, Roger. We'll talk at the airport."

"Right. See you shortly."

It was easy to spot the tall, silver haired Johns among the milling passengers. Roger waved. Evert nodded toward a noisy, dark cocktail lounge.

"I think we can order a sandwich here," Evert said by way of greeting.

They found a tiny table in the back of the smoking section. Neither man smoked. Evert began with small talk while they surveyed their surroundings.

"Well, Roger, it has been hard to get the Washington folks to focus beyond November's election. The administration absolutely is beleaguered by pressures for a peace dividend, and not just from the Democrats. The third party movement is a wild card. It's gathering strength. Everyone's speculating on what Perot, or any third party candidate, will mean in a tight race.

"The recessionary pressures we have in California continue to depress the economy, not only for the state, but for the entire country. The sprinkling of 'positive signs' are too fragile to leave a mark. Most of them dry up in all the political hot air before they hit the ground."

Evert warmed to his topic, Roger noticed, even if politics wasn't their reason for meeting. The waitress came, took their orders for two turkey sandwiches. Evert had black coffee. Roger ordered a glass of California Chardonnay. The Canby president leaned further forward in his seat and continued. Only Roger could hear him.

"It's to be expected. Our problem is to help the President and the Congress solve theirs. We need to get this nation going again. The American people are ready to do their part, but they need to be recognized as partners. Washington needs to level with them and work out all the elements of a long-range recovery plan. Americans can handle sophisticated concepts. We can handle belt-tightening. We want honesty."

Abruptly, without changing his position or voice, Johns changed the subject. "In all the time I've known you, Roger, never before have you insisted upon a face-to-face meeting. I know you wanted to see me before I left Oakland. I apologize for being so tied up. I did ask Phyllis if it were a life or death matter. She didn't let me off easy, so I figured I'd better take time from my meeting with the Department of Energy and the Commerce Secretary to see you."

"No problem, Ev. I knew I'd get a hearing. She doesn't know why I wanted to see you, though, at least, not specifically. She has a working knowledge of all my projects and how I have been allocating my time, however. Phyllis is very professional, one of the best."

He was going to say 'She's a nice lady,' but he'd been trying to be more sensitive to the way he used language about all females, including Carol, who was fond of pointing out his occasional sexist comments.

From his thin, leather portfolio, Roger Steadhold withdrew several sheets of yellow ruled paper. He had hand written the report. No one else had seen it. Their sandwiches arrived. Evert bit into his, probably wanting to enjoy part of his meal before hearing the bad news. It was bad news, of course. Good news, something like an important breakthrough, had a halo effect that transmitted brightly, nothing like that here. Evert looked at the papers in Roger's hand and swallowed. Roger's wine caused him to cough and push it aside. It was an inexpensive New York Gerwertz, not the Chardonnay he had ordered. Evert waited.

"Bottom line, Roger?"

"Shade Nettle has embezzled a million three, minimum, from Canby International."

Evert's head whipped back. He expressed no anger, but his eyes winced in pain. "If you're wrong, you are finished, Roger. You know that, so I'm sure you must have proof." He took the yellow sheets from Roger, gripped them in his hand. Roger nodded.

"Anything else?"

"Hsing Tom suspected something wrong. When he began closing in on the discrepancies, Shade had him transferred to Taipei."

"Hsing requested the transfer. His father was dying. Shade told me." He sighed. "Okay, I get it. What else?"

"Hsing didn't have anything concrete, but he pointed me in the right direction. Shona Oliver, the chief accountant, has taken some big risks for me, but Shade has cut her access. He may suspect her. Hsing's wife brought me his printouts of some of the accounts that needed to be scrutinized."

"His wife?" Evert frowned.

"She was just delivering some papers from Hsing. He wanted me to check out some things for him, as a trusted friend, but he didn't have anything specific, just several areas that needed a closer look. A jump in claims against the company, both insurance and a few in workers' comp that he couldn't nail down. Shade changed things around and reduced Hsings' oversight responsibilities when he became VP. Remember, Hsing was suspicious, but not absolutely positive of anything. He was trying to point to the areas he suspected. I didn't know what I had, to be honest. My investigative auditing skills weren't so great — they're better now — and I was busy, so I put the job off longer than I should have. Hell, his wife gave me the papers in February, months ago. I should have jumped right on it. When I did get around to wrestling with the problem, it took me forever to be sure of what it all meant, what I'm telling you tonight. Also, given the amounts and the methods used, others may be involved, probably very few. One, maybe two. I don't know who they are, if this is the case. That's why I asked for the 'face-to-face.'"

106

"Roger, I'll read this carefully when I have complete privacy." He folded the sheets into a thick packet and put them into his inside breast pocket. "I need some time to — to think about this. So many implications. Is there anything else?"

"No, I've outlined it all there. Some of my notes might be a bit cryptic. I'd planned to go through them with you."

"Let me go through what you've got. I'll get back to you. Anything else?"

"Can you tell me anything about Jake Hartig, not that he's connected to this. Just a feeling."

"I rated his work substandard on his last two performance reports, Roger. After the first one, I assigned Alice, one of our top executive secretaries to him, as you know. After the last review, I gave him six weeks. I probably should have replaced him on the spot. Anyway, I expect his letter of resignation no later than Monday. I'm planning to announce that Alice will be our new Director of Human Resources next Wednesday, if she'll agree. She should have had the job ten years ago. She's got to accept. Did you know that she and her husband were thinking of retiring? Going on the professional ballroom dancing circuit? What a waste."

Johns caught himself, "I mean what a tragedy for us at Canby, if we lose her. I blame myself for not paying more attention to our real talent. Someone works for years as a top manager but is classified and paid as a secretary. You get used to it, use their skills and take the credit. If we ever get things straightened out, will you help me do better in this area? I didn't expect anything like this — not my own people. Will you excuse me?" Evert Johns fumbled for his wallet, dropped a twenty on the table and turned to leave. He took a couple of steps and stopped, straightened and turned. He returned to the table. "You're a good man, Roger. I know this has been hard on you, too."

He clapped his hand on the younger man's shoulder. "Finish your sandwich and take care of this, will you? The twenty won't cover it. This is New York. Get some rest and I'll talk to you tomorrow. You going up to Boston?"

"As far as I know. Just to the Service Center and visit the European sales reps who are in New England for the week. Oh, also something about a briefing on the research on using sonar and sound to steer fish to the sea — salmon smolt runs.

"Salmon what?"

"Smolt — baby salmon, I assume. Might have some applications for the salmon and other fish in the California delta, keep 'em out of the pumps diverting water south. I don't have much of anything to go on. The briefing is by a Fort Lauderdale outfit. You didn't order this trip, did you? I received an urgent e-mail message from you, ostensibly, saying get on the next plane."

"No, I didn't order you here, or leave any instructions like that. We need to get a hold of Nettle. We'll get to the bottom of things tomorrow. Wing it, for now. This meeting didn't happen."

"Sure thing."

Roger watched the older man leave and forced himself to eat his sandwich. He sipped the sweet wine, but left it unfinished and caught a cab back to the hotel.

Deep in thought, he slammed the door on the cabby who was arguing for a bigger tip and headed for the hotel entrance. He swept by an imposing granite pillar which suddenly displayed a small flower with sharp petals radiating at random lengths. Before the image registered completely, Roger's brain telegraphed the searing pain of a smashed collarbone and the dizzying fall to the carpeted marble steps. A second flower blossomed on the granite, lower this time, but Roger didn't see this one. He heard no sound of shots, only the traffic noise from the busy street and the startled surprise of the doorman who rushed to his assistance.

The uniformed doorman knelt, rolled Roger over and saw the red stain growing out from under his suit up his white shirt collar. "Don't move. Someone around here just tried to kill you."

"Call an ambulance," the doorman barked at the parking attendant. "And the police."

"They're calling now, sir."

"Hang in there, buddy."

Roger became aware of the ambulance screeching and twisting its way through Manhattan. Dizzy with pain and fatigue, he fended off the attending paramedic until he extracted a promise from the bright, young face watching him to warn Evert Johns.

"He'll be landing at Dulles any moment. Canby International's Lear jet. Someone could shoot him too."

At the hospital, a lean, sharp-featured policeman's words broke into Roger's fog as he was rolled into surgery. Again, Roger tried to extract a promise to get a warning to Evert Johns. "My partner's making some calls right now. Don't worry," said the policeman.

# Chapter 13

.

When the twilight finally began to give the promise of darkness, the moon rose and dispelled it. Diane liked the night; its darkness was an asset that helped to hide them. She assumed any other humans would be enemies. Carol and Diane listened intently for any human sound. Their fright intensified without their being fully conscious of what was happening. They felt as if they were characters in a play or in some surreal world.

"Why are you so overly cautious about running into people? I understand about our kidnappers, but anybody else would help us," Carol said.

"Hunters. Some legal and some illegal. When we camped on the delta, we would occasionally run into guys who would drive out on the deserted levees in the middle of the night and shoot at anything that moved."

Then, realizing Carol's alarm, she quickly added. "It only happened twice. We'll be fine."

Diane explained that they would be climbing in and out of the water more than once. They dressed by putting their jackets over their underwear and moved from their hiding place, each carrying a plastic bag. Fortuitously, they both had worn dark jackets.

Carol ran down the steep levee and into the cornfield, followed after a minute by Diane, who had been watching and listening for anything unusual. They began following a wide furrow across the field, according to plan. Ragged edged leaves grabbed them in scratchy, crackling embraces. Dry, sandy loam squished between their toes. Turning almost completely sideways, the women struggled along the furrow. There was little room for them among the tightly spaced rows of stalks. The tall plants had tasseled and hid the women easily. The corn appeared almost ready for harvest. Pollen sprinkled down onto their heads. Diane stifled a sneeze. They came to a wider furrow where they could walk out of the reach of the slapping plants. Two-thirds of the way across the field, they heard an automobile engine on the levee somewhere far to their right. They couldn't tell exactly where. Without a word, each woman stepped from the furrow and forced her way into the row of corn stalks, their bare feet struggling with the roots for space into the rich, soft, soil. Some of the plants gave way. Saw-edged leaves scratched at their bodies. The engine stopped. A door slammed then came the tortuous sound of metal against metal and rushing water.

"Irrigating," Carol said. Diane nodded agreement.

They both resumed breathing normally.

"A farmer! He could help us." Carol started running along the wide furrow. "Help! Help!"

Diane waited. Two blasts from a shotgun rang out in the night. Buckshot rained down all around, sounding like hail on the corn.

"Carol, get down!"

"That bastard's shooting at us."

"Shut up and hide."

Obscenities accompanied the third blast over the field.

"He doesn't know where we are," Carol whispered.

"I don't think he's too thrilled about finding someone in his field. Probably figures we're stealing his corn."

"I was yelling for hel—." Another blast and more buckshot rain.

"He can't see us and can't hear what you were yelling over all that noise. Maybe when he turns the water off, but that'll be hours."

"No thanks. I'm not going any closer to that creep. He's probably going to get his AK-47."

With a departing blast over the field, the farmer climbed back into his vehicle and drove away. Carol and Diane continued toward their original target. When they reached the open space between the corn and the next levee, Diane picked two ears of corn. "Let's eat first."

"Raw?"

"It should be great, real sweet. The reason farmers carry shotguns."

While edible, the corn was a big disappointment. It looked like any other corn, but it had no flavor at all.

"So much for that theory. Maybe it's seed corn or maybe feed for cattle," Diane said.

Carol finished her second ear and shot her that funny glance again. "Cattle," she said, and nodded her head as if she understood or cared.

Buzzing mosquitoes tormented them, attacking in swarms. A bullfrog began its chorus. "Oh my God. What's that?" Carol asked.

"Bullfrog."

"You're kidding. Sounds like a dying cow. I want to get out of here. Let's get going."

"Here, husk these. See, the frog quit. He's afraid of us."

They husked and packed four more ears into the plastic bundles, trying to ensure that they wouldn't puncture the bags and climbed the levee near a stunted willow. No road atop this one. They waited in the shadows watching and listening. Mount Diablo was visible in the moonlight. Far to the east, a tractor could be heard working a field. Occasionally, the sounds of a beer party wafted to them when an air current was just right. It seemed to be exactly in the direction they wanted to go, but at quite a distance. From the top of the levee they started to climb down to a narrow strip of ground along the shore.

Heavy, uneven chunks of concrete had been dumped along this section in an attempt to stop erosion of the bank. Even with the bright moon, it was rough going. The concrete tore at their feet and hands. A loud splash came from somewhere out in the middle. Carol jumped.

"Fish," Diane said.

"I realize that, but I'm scared of what's hiding around these rocks. Every time I put down a hand or a foot, I feel a snake's going to bite me."

A small cloud drifted across part of the moon. The night was hot. The women shed their jackets. In just their underwear again, they carefully checked their bundles. Diane had thrown a small, leafy branch as far out into the water as she could and watched it swirl in an eddy before being captured by the current. The wind could blow one way and the current be headed another, she knew, but there was barely any breeze now. Strong currents moved through these waters driven naturally by the tidal action of the coastal bays miles and miles to the west and artificially by the huge pumping stations pulling the water out of the system into the canals and tunnels south to the Los Angeles basin. This slough was wider than the one they had left on the other side of the cornfield, but Diane hoped they wouldn't have any trouble swimming across to the clump of brush they had selected.

The best Diane could tell, the twig had drifted rapidly toward what she thought was up river. One couldn't really be sure with the tangle of channels and sloughs running in all directions. When the cloud drifted away from the moon, the women were a third of the way across, swimming a kind of combination side-stroke dog paddle, trying to keep the bundles above water. The water was cool and welcome after the hot day and the warm, mosquito-filled night. It soothed Diane's bruises, but it was tiring. The current that carried the twig now caught them and carried them too. Taking care not to wear themselves out

113

fighting it too much, Carol and Diane missed their original target but came ashore at a small sandy beach area. It was just as well.

The shadowy clump of bushes and trees they had selected for their original target was one of the numerous thick, impenetrable masses of blackberry vines that grow throughout the delta. On the tiny beach where they came ashore, they rested. Blackberries crowded in on them from one side here, too, thick willows and underbrush on the other. The bank of the levee was steep and impossible to climb. At some time, a part of this high earthen barrier must have given way and collapsed, creating the small, smooth patch of sand. They tried to climb up onto the top of the levee, but there was no solid footing, not even giving each other a foot up helped.

"Well, we can go back into the water and look for a better spot or we can try to go up through the bushes," Diane said. "What do you think?"

"Let's try the bushes again. Maybe we can get enough of a hold to work our way up the edge."

They struggled. The bushes scraped and scratched them. One of their smaller plastic bags snagged, then shredded, spewing its contents. They stopped to regroup. Afraid the corn would be too heavy and might poke holes in the remaining bags, they ate the remaining ears even though they weren't hungry. They started again.

Diane pulled herself up with the help of a sturdy willow branch. Ants, invisible in the night, were running up and down the bark, drawn by the sweet, sticky sap. They began biting, stinging her tender forearm. She moved faster. Carol followed right behind her. Grasping about for another handhold, Diane next encountered something soft but very strong. Her hand closed on a thin branch, and a rusty fishhook bit into the flesh of her right palm between her thumb and forefinger.

"Damn. Fishhook. Oh, shit. Ow!"

She tentatively pulled at the hook in her hand. Her footing was slipping. Carol threw herself to one side, out of her way, to avoid being pushed all the way back down the bank. A branch clawed at the back of her neck. Diane caught herself and tested the unseen line again. It tugged on the hook in her hand.

"What's happening? You okay?" Carol asked.

"Trying to bite through the damn line." She positioned the line precisely between her front teeth. She had begun to fear for her teeth when the line broke.

"What's the hold up?" Impatience filtered Carol's voice.

"I got a fishhook in my hand."

"Oh — "

"I need to pull it through."

"Oh, geez! Can I help?"

"Get me a corner of one of the jackets, something to grip it with. My fingers are getting caught on all the damn barbs."

To regain some control over her thoughts, Diane began to deliberately think only about the immediate, the next few minutes. She shut out the next day, the next hour. Only their next move mattered. With a series of piercing yelps, Diane pulled the hook through her flesh.

\*   \*   \*

In Japan, Diane's husband spoke to a machine across the Pacific in California.

"Hi, honey. It's Brad. I'm sorry I've missed you. I just wanted to hear your voice. It looks like a couple more weeks here, at least. We're working long, long hours — until we can't see straight any longer — pretty boring routine. My room is spartan, only the essentials, not a place where you would want to spend any extra time.

"When I first arrived, I went to see the local sights in and around Gifu and took some pictures. I bought you a present for your Ikebana. I have found a couple of good Japanese fast food places. It helps that I love Japanese food.

"Don't try to reach me unless it's an emergency. I'm just here in the room to sleep between the long sessions at the installation. I'll try to reach you again in a day or two. Time is starting to run together over here. I miss you. If this goes on much longer, see if you can clear your schedule and fly over. Check that. There's not too much to do, and I have to work the whole time. Bad idea, I guess. Take care. I love you, Honey. Bye."

\* \* \*

At New York's John F. Kennedy Airport, two security guards took their 2:15 am coffee break near the main drop-off point for international passengers. They chatted and watched the people. They had been placed on high alert, half an hour earlier, something about a call from the FBI. Passengers dribbled toward the concourse for a Swissair flight that was being announced. They saw a big man dump a heavy plastic bag into a trashcan. Nettle might not have attracted their attention, if he hadn't glanced around. He moved his head in little quick motions, spotted the security officers, stared, then reddened. He moved away hurriedly, on his way to the waiting area at the gate.

"We might have a live one over there," said one guard to the other.

"Yeah, we might." The second guard laughed a pretend laugh, as if they were joking. They maintained their casual posture, knowing the man they watched could not hear them. After a couple of moments, one guard stood, semi-shielding the other who spoke into his radio. A guard at the passenger screening area took the message and kept Nettle in view. Within three minutes a janitor rode up to the trash can on a small, motorized vehicle fitted with smaller two trash cans. The janitor bounced from his cart, trash bag in hand, and proceeded to empty the receptacle where Shade had deposited his gun. The janitor completed his task, jumped back into his cart. As he sped away, he pulled the radio from his belt and held it close to his mouth.

\* \* \*

116

Something had gone wrong. Jake Hartig nosed around the office all afternoon, his frustration and agitation reaching the explosive point. No one seemed to know why Steadhold was ordered to the East Coast without any notice, and where the hell was Nettle? He was supposed to be here — especially today. Checking for messages on his second line at home, he learned that Rudy and his friend had Roger's wife. Now what? This was Nettle's idea.

Not knowing what else to do, Jake stayed at the office until nine, long after everyone on the floor had gone. Nettle did not call. There was no word of any kind. Only a machine answered when Jake called his house.

Finally, Jake left the building, took a couple of wrong turns driving home, not sure he wanted to go home, not knowing where to go. What should he tell those guys when they called back at midnight? Stopped at an unusually long signal, he pulled out the east Oakland address of Al Gonzales that he had copied from Roger's little green notebook. He pulled over and decided to see if he could locate the place on his map. It didn't look too far, so he would drive by. It proved a bit more difficult to find, driving through the neighborhoods, but he found Humbolt Street eventually and began checking the numbers. The last block had to be the one where Gonzales lived, but there was a block party winding down. Hartig felt conspicuous, too many people around to notice him and his car, so he headed back to Thirty-fifth Avenue and the highlands. He didn't even know what Gonzales looked like. What was he thinking? But his mind still convulsed.

The City of Oakland emergency van was the last one to leave the wide residential street where crews had repaired a damaged water pipe that had threatened to flood a couple of homes on the downhill side. The driver was alone, closing the back door after getting the last of the gear packed up. Jake pulled up opposite him and called out, "Can you wait a minute? I live here. I want to ask you something."

The weary worker shrugged and waited by the open door of the driver's side for Jake to park. Pretending to blow his nose,

Jake partially covered his face with his handkerchief. He moved in close, too close into the man's personal space. Too late, the city worker saw the gun.

"Hey, Mister, I'm just —"

"Open the back. Get in."

"There's no room."

"Get in, feet first with your head toward the door."

The man did so. Jake struck a savage blow to the man's head dazing him. Hartig appropriated some thin insulated wire and orange plastic stripping tape to secure the man's hands. The head wound bled profusely. Jake hoped he hadn't killed the guy, then decided he didn't care. He took the keys from the man's overalls, closed the door, climbed into the driver's seat and drove away.

Haunted by the closed-mouthed treatment he had received from Janet and Phyllis, even from Alice, his own secretary, Jake drove to Shade Nettle's home in Piedmont. He thought the city van would let him watch the house without raising as much suspicion as his car might. The secretaries told him that Johns was in Washington, and Steadhold was in New York. The women could not, or would not, tell him anything about why Steadhold left so hurriedly. At least he wasn't in the same city with Johns, but it sure loused up the plan Jake had set in motion for Steadhold.

Years ago, Jake Hartig had heard the rumor that Nettle was a Swiss citizen. A quick check of Nettle's personnel file confirmed its truth. Jake drove by the Nettle's home twice, but he didn't see the black Lexus. Of course, it could be in the garage.

Jake parked and pondered what he'd done. Possibility after possibility jumbled into his mind, none of them good. He fidgeted with the steering wheel, his moustache, the top of his baldhead. Certainly not his usual coolness in a crisis, he realized, but he couldn't stop. Where the hell was Nettle? Deep in the pit of his gut, he had the feeling Nettle had dealt him out.

The guy in the back started moving around, banging things with his feet and groaning. "Quiet back there!" Jake said. He hardly noticed the high-pitched sound of his own voice. He had

118

missed the midnight call from the kidnappers, but didn't know what to tell them, anyhow.

Hartig regained a measure of his senses and returned the truck to its original spot, left the city worker in the back, hoping he wouldn't be able to identify him. Jake hurriedly tried to wipe his fingerprints off the inside of the utility vehicle. He retrieved his car and headed for his apartment. There still was his letter of resignation to do before Monday.

"I resign," signed Jake Hartig. Jake resented making the firing easy for Johns. The president had said, "I'm permitting you to resign, Jake. Come up with some plausible reason." Jake decided to make Evert Johns come up with his own face-saving reasons.

But Jake snapped before Monday.

# Chapter 14

Away from the water, looking in the direction of the landmark mountain of the coastal range, Carol and Diane could see another cultivated field. This one had something smaller than corn, tomatoes or peppers, maybe — no cover, only cloud shadows for hiding. The night was hot, but wet from their swim; they didn't feel too warm. Carol held out her arm in line with Mount Diablo, and tried to take a bearing on a darker outline, indistinguishable among many, on the moonlit levee across the field.

"We should skirt this field along the base of the levee," Diane suggested. "It will take longer, but we can hide among the shadows if we have to. Walking along the top of the levee, we would stand out too easily against this night sky."

The climb down the levee to the field was farther, but much easier, than the climb from the water had been. In just over fifteen minutes, they had skirted one end of the field, reached the point they thought was about right, and scampered up the levee to take another sighting. Diane's hand throbbed. Moonlight was still good, but the waterway before them was wider than the last one, and the wind had picked up slightly. In spite of their exertion, they were becoming chilled. A crippled, young poplar slumped toward the river from the levee, its top most branches dead sticks. They were hard, brittle and sharp. The living branches were pliable and still had some leaves. Diane and Carol braced themselves with help from the dying tree and descended to the water's edge, trying not to rely too much on the poor tree, for fear that it might pull completely loose from the bank.

"Ready for another swim?" Diane asked. "This one will be a little tougher than the last one."

"Okay, at least the mosquitoes quit."

"It's the breeze."

"Huh?"

"Let's stop a few minutes. Do we still have that bottle of aspirin? We'll split the soda now so we don't have to lug it across the river."

Carol fished into the bag, produced the soda, the aspirin and the can of Spam. Handing the aspirin to Diane, she popped open the Pepsi.

"I could use a couple of those too," she said after Diane counted out three of the flaky tablets. "Aspirin and Pepsi — never tried that combination before. We could open the Spam. Bet you wouldn't even notice the aspirin in that."

"Let's save it until we really need it," Diane said after clumsily swallowing the three aspirin. They were disintegrating in her throat.

She was worrying about where they were, her early optimism failing along with her strength, but she forced herself to lay out a strategy for this crossing.

"Don't worry about drifting off course as we swim this one. We're going to drift with the current, just like the last one, only more. We do need to get across, though." Diane squeezed the top of the grocery bag around her finger, making a small air hole and began blowing air into the bag. She then twisted the bag closed and tied the handles back together again and put it inside the larger garbage bag which she also tried to fill with air.

"This will be more of a problem on this crossing, but come daylight, we definitely will need our clothes — wet or not."

Suddenly, Carol asked, "We could drown this time, couldn't we?"

"Yes, we could."

Irrational as it was to attempt another crossing in the night, this one wider, with a stronger current than the last one, their compulsion to put great distance between themselves and the houseboat forced the women on.

"We may regret it, but I'm dumping the Spam. The can's a little puffy and it adds weight," Carol said.

"That's okay. Can you help me with this? It might float." Diane struggled with a huge waterlogged tree limb, half submerged at the water's edge. With difficulty, they worked it free, but it didn't float, at least not entirely, not enough to support the two of them. Tired, they didn't bother to pull it back onto the beach. Diane knew she had created a boating hazard, especially if it floated out towards the middle, just beneath the surface, but the delta was full of boating hazards. They sat down on the ground where Diane had left the bag.

"Carol, you want the water wing or should I wear it?"

"What?"

"Whoever takes the bag across can keep both hands free if we tie this thing to the back of a bra strap."

"Oh. Okay, I'll do it." Carol said carelessly, not caring much any more.

Diane tied the remainder of the plastic bag handles in a granny knot to the back of Carol's bra. She had intended to tie a square knot but couldn't see in the dim light.

It must be very late, she thought. "Let's wade out and move along the shoreline. We need to find something that will help us float in case we get too tired to swim the whole way."

"Okay." Carol spoke with little conviction.

They stumbled, tripped and fell into sudden deep spots. Visibility was terrible, especially trying to distinguish a log or limb that would float, one they could manage to free from all the rest of the tangled foliage. They traveled a considerable distance, each beginning to worry about getting off the course line with

Mount Diablo they had set. It was Carol who first spotted the patch of white in the fast waning moonlight.

"Diane, look! What's that?"

"Let's go see."

They waded carefully into shore. It was an old Styrofoam cooler with a small hole in the bottom, no top and battered down sides. It stank, but it would float. Diane rinsed it out vigorously. Carol climbed up to the top of the levee, an easier climb here than the last one, and continued to search for anything else that would float. She found a large piece of Styrofoam that might have been the lid to the cooler, and a board. She almost discarded the board but thought again and returned with it to where Diane was analyzing the possibilities of how to best use the cooler.

"Good job," said Diane. "Do we still have our pantyhose in the bag?"

Carol had repacked after the first bag split, spilling everything it contained in the thicket. "I think so."

Untying and unpacking turned up both pair of pantyhose. They took out one pair, repacked, retied, and reattached the bag to the back of Carol's bra. They didn't bother to blow it up, deciding it was wasted effort. Diane carefully began to break apart the cooler using both feet to push out one side, then another, then carefully breaking off the remaining two sides until she had four larger pieces and scraps. The board Carol found was twice as large as the largest piece of Styrofoam. It took the two of them to break it in two, which they did with the help of a large, uneven rock. With all the pieces close to the same size, the women set about arranging them in the most advantageous alignment. They discarded one of the pieces of wood, but kept the other and used the pantyhose to tie it with the cooler pieces into a kind of thick kickboard like the ones children use when they're learning to swim. Although the air was still warm, it was cooling, and the women shivered while they worked.

"Let's kick out as far as we can," Diane said. "All the way across, if possible. More likely, the current will catch us and carry us a good ways, like last time. Just be sure to hang onto this thing. I hope this will keep us both afloat, if we're caught in the current. We're miles and miles from the shipping channel. This waterway will take all kinds of twists and turns, so sooner or later we'll reach shore." I hope, she thought to herself.

Gingerly, they waded out to the drop-off point in the warm, dark water. The women were two-thirds the way across when the current suddenly spun them around and began persistently moving them downstream in spite of their coordinated efforts to reach the bank.

"Hang on! I think I drank half the river," Carol sputtered, swallowing more.

Their efforts now became concentrated on staying afloat rather than getting across. The setting moon no longer lit the surface of the water. No clouds now, but the darkness was closing in on them. They each had an arm across the makeshift float and used their other arm for balance and steering, although they had little idea of where to steer. They just tried to face in the direction the water swept them. The current increased. The river curved. Diane noticed a small red light ahead, high above them. Carol saw it too. In the moment they realized what it was it was too late.

The superstructure of a bridge loomed out of the darkness. The two, ugly, wide cement footings were easier to see, but the women had been looking at the red warning light high above.

"Kick," Diane screamed.

They hit the stanchion full force, slamming up against the hard cement. Their float crumbled and fell away in tiny pieces. Carol found a ridge and hung on. Diane hit so hard that she was stunned momentarily. Carol grasped one of her arms. Diane bobbed under but came up quickly, trying to get her free hand onto something. Then her foot found the slippery ledge underwater and her hand the ridge that Carol was grasping.

Doggedly, the women clung there, their bodies breaking the water that swept under the bridge. It was a narrow railroad bridge, not one for automobiles. No help here. No one around.

Diane, unaware of her own trembling with all the water splashing over her head, waited until her breathing returned to something like normal. She put her mouth close to Carol's head yelled. "Try to stay together. Try to get to that side. Ready?"

"Ready!"

They clasped hands, each leaving one hand free, inched forward one tiny step. Carol slipped, let go and was gone. The next instant the river plucked Diane away. She screamed. The river tore the women into the full force of the current again. Pulled under for several yards, each struggled for her life.

Surfacing in less tumultuous waters, and finding each other, they tried to beat back panic. The water still bore them along, but the speed had slowed. The river was quiet again. Thinking they might be in an eddy or in shallow water, Diane tried to touch bottom, too deep. She kept trying every so often. She was rewarded on her fourth try when her knee, not just a toe, struck soft mud.

"Carol, Carol," she called. "Over here."

For a moment, there was no response. Diane was in dark shadows. Carol couldn't see her.

"Carol! Over here!"

"Diane?"

"Here, Carol," Diane splashed to make her position more obvious.

Carol swam toward the sound. She almost beached herself, not realizing she had reached shallow water.

"Carol, you can stand up here," Diane said, moving toward her friend.

Carol was breathing hard. She knelt in the submerged mud, gathering her strength before trying to stand.

They had reached the shallows, but they couldn't get near the levee here. Blackberry brambles overhung the water's edge in huge tangles. The women had to keep wading. It seemed a considerable distance. Walking along the levee would be much faster, if they could only get up there. The soft mud gave way to a mud-sand mixture, then back to sticky, sucking mud again.

Gradually, they came upon firmer footing, only once in a while did their feet sink up to the ankle. The greater hazards were the holes and sharp objects of all kinds that poked and scratched at their bare feet. Moving slowly, not talking, they made very little noise. They heard no other human sounds, only an occasional bullfrog and insects, especially crickets whose chirping filled the darkness with life.

Finally Diane spoke. "Crickets are lucky."

"According to whom?"

"The Japanese believe they are. I agree with them. That's why cricket cages are so popular. Many Japanese homes have pet crickets."

"Whatever."

The blackberry brambles gave way at last to a thicket of bamboo, over eight feet tall. There was room to leave the water and stand on a tiny beach, but like the blackberry vines, there was no penetrating the bamboo. It was too thick and the mature stalks too large to push out of the way. The women resumed their wading. Somewhere ahead a loud splash abruptly stopped them.

"Fish jumped," Diane whispered.

"Sounded like a whale," Carol said.

"Probably up there where the starlight is playing on the water. It's a good omen."

"Humph, not for the fish's dinner it wasn't. Probably a cricket dinner."

The bamboo thinned and disappeared. They continued their cautious wading. The levee appeared quite steep. They couldn't see very well.

Around a leaning tree they came to an indention in the bank and an area that appeared somewhat worn down. They waded into shore without a word, moving on separate paths.

Carol yelled in pain through gritted teeth, trying desperately not to make noise. "My foot — I'm really hurt, Diane. Something's ripped open my foot. Oh, God. Feels like a saw blade or broken glass. Oh, God. Oh, God."

Diane turned and, arm outstretched, moved toward her. Carol was in trouble.

"Stay there," Carol commanded. "I've cut my foot badly. Be careful." She was calm, wounded, but calm.

"Can you get to the beach?"

"If there's no more sharp stuff." She moved gingerly testing each step with her foot before putting weight on it. She drew alongside Diane.

Dear God, help us get though this, Diane prayed silently, taking Carol's right arm over her shoulder and wrapping her left arm around Carol's waist to help her out of the water. Diane thought about the sand, mud and microorganisms burrowed into Carol's flesh, propelled by ugly, uneven razor sharp edges.

Sitting on the tiny beach, they couldn't see much. The foot was bleeding, but not pumping blood. "Do you think there's any glass left in the cuts?" Diane asked.

"Don't think so."

Diane reached for Carol's foot. "Damn it. Don't touch me!" With both hands, Carol probed her own foot. Diane could see her teeth biting into her lower lip. "Feels awful, but I don't think there are any pieces in it. It felt like I stepped onto something wedged into the bottom, something really solid. It feels like two gashes, one wrapped around my instep, not too deep. The other runs from under my two smallest toes around then all the way down the outside edge. Oh, God."

Diane fished blindly though the plastic bag. She found what she was searching for and pulled out the other pair of pantyhose. Taking the body portion, she folded it twice and using the two legs, began wrapping them in opposite directions around the foot. Carol said nothing this time.

"Too tight?" she asked when she felt Carol wince.

"I guess not. We'll see when I try to walk on it."

"That's the spirit. We're going to get out of all this, Carol. I promise."

Diane found the aspirin bottle, opened the childproof lid with her teeth and poured out the crumbs of the last three aspirin.

"Take these." She brought the aspirin pieces up to Carol's mouth. "I don't want to drop them. They'd be gone forever. Sorry there's nothing to wash it down with."

Carol cupped her hand under her mouth and opened wide. "How about a handful of water?"

"No. You really don't want to drink the river water, Carol. Try to work up some spit."

"I must have swallowed gallons of water when we hit the bridge. A little more can't hurt."

"Forget what you swallowed before. It's too late for that. Don't drink any more if you can help it, not even a handful."

"Ugh. The aspirin's so terrible, maybe it'll take my mind off my foot."

"Look. Out there, something on the water," Diane pointed into the darkness. "Ducks?" They watched a darker shadow moving across the water midstream. It disappeared, then reappeared. "Could be Mergansers, but I think it's too early for their migration."

"I hate you, Diane! I hate this place! Hell, shit, damn! My foot hurts! Damn the ducks! The mud! The mosquitoes, the stickers. What are you, a super crazy Girl Scout?" She fingered a stinging cut along its course from behind her ear to the back of her neck.

"It's better than being dead, Miss Manners. Let's go." Diane hauled Carol to her feet and shoved her closer to the levee. Tears and snot on Carol's face glistened in the starlight.

They struggled up the levee, beginning what was to be a two and a half-mile trek. On top of the levee, they found a road of hard dirt and loose rocks. It was impossible to see what crop was in the field below, but across the water they could discern that the slough was very wide with a long, thin island running its full length. Diane thought she recognized the slough. The women with their pathetic bag of wet clothes, hobbled along like a three-legged racer in slow motion, but they made progress. The exertion helped fend off the cold. The night air was warm, but fatigue and the water had started to chill them again.

"Where's a hot flash when you need it," Diane mumbled, stifling a sneeze, from the cool air this time, instead of her allergies.

The road turned ninety degrees to the left. "Wait here a second," Diane said. She left Carol and headed to the levee's edge. She moved up and down the levee searching for a good place to climb down. When she came back, she led Carol down the levee and into the water again. This time they swam straight across, and waded carefully along the opposite bank, making no attempt to climb this levee.

"I can't swim anymore. Please stop," Carol said. "Let's wait here until morning."

"I know where we are," Diane whispered excitedly. She moved faster, with greater conviction. "There's a marina not too far."

"Can't we rest first?"

"There's no resting place until we get across. Besides, we're wet now."

"How many more times will we have to swim? I'm getting tired."

"I can't remember exactly. We always had a boat when we were here. The water was our road."

"Diane, how can you be so sure you know where we are? It's dark. All these levees look the same. I don't want to get cut again."

Rifle shots rang out in the distance, from across the large tract they had crossed. Diane grabbed Carol around the waist. They struggled out to the deep water and began to swim. They spoke no more. There was a current, but it was weaker than before. Diane swam a sort of modified breaststroke and was making steady progress when she sensed Carol was not with her. She stopped, turned to look back. She could see Carol's head, a solid black silhouette against the motion of the moving ebony of the surface which occasionally flashed a pale reflection of starlight. Diane started back toward her. Carol's head disappeared. There was no sound, no splash. She was just gone.

"Carol!"

Diane took three wild strokes to where she thought Carol went under. Her foot struck something and she dove under. She caught hold of some fingers and then some hair. Diane strengthened her grip on the hair and surfaced. Carol didn't resist, but she started to cough. She spread her arms wide and tried to keep herself afloat. Diane was too worried to leave her to her own devices. She turned Carol over, slipped her hand under Carol's chin and started swimming, praying the adrenal rush would last.

The weaker current nevertheless carried the women beyond the point Diane had set. It was a small white frame structure situated back on a wider section of the levee with just the tops of the windows and the roofline visible from the water — probably a small house. A dog barked.

Diane could hear the creak of a dock or a mooring of some sort, but the women were too far from it to get to it. The dog continued to bark from somewhere up on the levee. They drifted past only a third of the way out, but they each would have to have been swimming strongly to make the levee or the dock. Diane remembered another slough coming into the main channel that should be just ahead. There used to be a couple of small beaches, one on the corner, one to her left, if it was slack or low tide. There were no beaches that she could recall on the tract of land where the dog was, but she was willing to settle for any solid ground. Trying to use the current, Diane was pulling with all her strength, hoping to intersect the levee across Italian Slough. She believed they were at the intersection of Italian Slough and Old River. Oh, please, please make it be Italian Slough and Old River.

Yes, it was! Everything she expected was there. Excitement fired her ebbing strength. Carol tried to say something and started to stroke the water in assistance, but Diane didn't loosen her hold on her chin. Carol tried again to say she was all right now.

"Diane," cough, "I'm okay."

Diane hesitated.

"I can swim on my own."

Diane released her, "Stay with me. It's not far, right straight ahead."

Carol didn't answer. She was swimming.

The two bedraggled creatures crawled out of the water, collapsed on the tiny sand beach. The droopy, white grocery bag was still attached to the back of Carol's bra. With the air gone, it had been extra weight, but at least it wasn't full of water.

"This is Italian Slough and Old River," Diane said. "We're going to make it. We used to launch our boat not far from here. There's a marina where we can get help."

They curled where they were and fell asleep. Most of an hour passed before either stirred. Another hour passed. A noise woke them. Neither moved. They held their breath, waiting — nothing, just small animals of the night moving about. Carol reached over and touched Diane who squeezed her hand in reply. They got up slowly, keeping silent. The stars were very dim now, the sky dark gray instead of black. Carol retied the makeshift pantyhose bandage, tightening it around her foot.

The levee they climbed this time consisted of loose sand. They climbed relatively easily, but the sand worked its way painfully into the cuts on Carol's foot. They resumed the now familiar pattern of wait, watch, listen, go. Another narrow, dirt road ran along the top of this levee. Their hobbling along on three good legs was more practiced now, but hardly the speed either of them could have walked under normal circumstances.

In the east, faint hints of pink and gold sunbeams began to chase the trailing gray cloak of night. Far ahead, somewhere in a waterway they couldn't see, a big one hundred horsepower Merc shattered the quiet as it turned over and started. The boat idled for some time, moving down the distant slough, then roared to life at full throttle. As the ominous sound sped toward them, the women crouched to hide. It didn't matter. The fisherman skipped along the surface with only the heavy motor bringing the hull back into contact with the water, every several yards. He headed toward Old River and turned right, sped along and took a wide turn left before cutting his speed. He headed back along the route the women had come.

After the wake crashed into the banks on either side and died away, Carol and Diane moved again. Faint light covered half the sky now. Purple joined the gold and pink of the dawn. The night retreated to the base of Mount Diablo where its flight was interrupted momentarily. The birds, rudely awakened and bounced by the passing boat, began their songs to the morning.

At a sharp turn, along the top of the levee, Carol and Diane paused to take in the changing sky, over the horizon, the sun's spark to the wick of the Earth's atmosphere. A mockingbird began to review its catalogue of songs. It was Carol this time who tugged at Diane to move on. Diane turned quickly to her, alert, then relaxed, when she saw Carol's smile and nod toward the road. The dawn brought a rare semblance of normalcy.

"Tell me something," Carol said as they began walking.

"Sure. What?"

"You're on one of the governor's advisory committees —"

"Chapter 2. We advise on the allocation of federal funds that California receives. Doesn't mean the governor has to listen."

"Whatever. How'd you get the appointment? How did you really get it?"

"Like every other appointee. It's either personal connections or major contributions, or both. I have a good friend on the State Board of Education. Kio Yashikawa recommended me when the governor's staff asked him for a name. I think they were coming up short, and I had the background the law required. Kio mentioned I covered a two or three slots for them, board member, high school and college teacher."

"Why did he recommend you?"

"I will tell you, but this is a private conversation." Diane waited for Carol's nod of consent. "Kio knows community colleges inside out, but has only surface knowledge of K-12. He's bright, learning all the time. But, at first, he had little understanding of the issues, the needs, the curriculum reforms. I was the one he would call for a concise rundown of those issues. We had been colleagues, both good teachers. We respect each other, even though we argue over educational philosophy."

"Why did you help him, if you didn't agree with him?"

"Having all the facts may not guarantee a good decision, but not having them is worse."

"You didn't contribute big bucks to the governor's campaign?"

"No, I don't always agree with him, either."

"I assume you left that part off the application papers?"

Diane smiled. "Right. They didn't ask that, just what party I was."

"Doesn't sound like the usual way someone gets an appointment." Carol sounded preoccupied.

"There are twelve of us. I would guess at least three or four, maybe more, bought their appointments. There's the usual north/south and valley/rural verses the coastal/urban distribution. Everyone has some sort of credentials for — Well, I not sure about a couple."

They talked as if they were driving to Sacramento, not fleeing their kidnappers. They followed the road around the turn. The slough narrowed. The breeze was almost imperceptible. No other boats intruded. The cover along the road thinned, then disappeared. Someone approaching from any direction would see them easily now. The heavy fear of their reality returned to nibble at the edges of their minds. Diane helped Carol down the levee on the water side, where they would not stand out along the horizon. She undid the "bandage" and examined the open slashes on Carol's foot.

"Looks like hell," she said, repositioning the pantyhose and tying up the foot again.

"You look like Bride of Frankenstein, speaking of looking like hell," Carol said. "Your whole face is red, even where you aren't bruised. Looks painful, too."

"Not real bad, unless I bump my hand or touch my face. It's all the bites and scratches. They're giving me fits." But Diane's fingers went instinctively to her left cheekbone, up along her eye, then down around her nose. Each place she touched hurt. She had the sensation of loose webbing ripping apart under the surface of her skin. On her hand the area between her right thumb and forefinger was puffy and oozing from the fishhook wound. When was her last tetanus shot? Probably twenty years ago, she thought. Great. "We both are going to need tetanus shots when we get back," she said. "I sure could use a drink of water."

"I swallowed more water during that last swim. Couldn't help it," Carol said.

"Carol, you really don't want to drink this stuff unless it has been boiled at least ten minutes, treated with chlorine or both."

Debris floated on the glassy surface, small dark matter interspersed with fluffy white. The breeze was not rippling the water, yet the debris drifted closer. Diane was collecting her thoughts. They needed to move, to get to the marina. She saw Carol studying the water and begin retching with violent dry heaves. Toilet paper and human waste floated closer. Diane grabbed Carol's arm and yanked her back up to the road. "Come on. Let's go!"

Carol ran without regard to her sore foot. A brutal lesson, thought Diane. Someone was awake upstream in one of the old houseboats or camping, or who knows what. But with Carol running on her own, they were making better time. Dark red blotches decorated every other footprint when she slowed to a gimpy, fast walk.

# Chapter 15

The sun rose in the eastern sky, and soft, golden light filled the quivering air and landscape. The fanciful spectacle of first light raced away leaving the sideways angle of the sun's rays setting fire to the land, casting long, dark fingers from the bamboo clumps and tall, scrawny weeds. Even the small rocks and dead grasses along the berm of the levee had their role in the play of tawny light and shadow. The warm night air insured no mist rose from the water's surface. To the west, Mount Diablo floated above a thin line of cloudy haze, bright and animated. The mountain sparkled and winked at them.

In the distance, a paved road ran perpendicular to where Diane paused to silently absorb the morning's beauty. Off to the left, across the slough were some haphazard structures, old housing for farm workers. A rusting, abandoned flatbed truck rested on its axles. The small barracks-like buildings seemed deserted. Beyond these, entering at a right angle, was another small slough. Everything was quiet except the red-tailed hawk, circling overhead with its compelling, rhythmic morning calls. On the opposite bank, running parallel with them, Diane and Carol could see a short, low trestle past the structures, beyond the trestle, trees and a couple of long mobile homes with TV antennas.

"There's the marina," Diane said, pointing in the direction of the mobile home on the levee beyond the trestle.

"You couldn't tell it by me. That ramshackle place? Where do they keep the boats?"

"In the parking lot. You can't see much from here. Not many people keep their boats at this place. Too dusty and windy and hot. People don't keep their boats in the water here. The docks are just for loading and unloading."

"I don't see any docks."

"They're up that arm to the left beyond the railroad bridge. We'll go across when we are even with the far side of the trestle. If we were to go across here, we'd have to cross a second time to reach the launch ramp, just once if we cross further up."

"Turds! Human turds, complete with toilet paper! Raw sewage! I'm not going in that water again! Why not go out to that road and follow it back and into the marina?" Carol stamped her foot. "Ow!"

"It's farther than it looks, several miles. Keep your voice down. Sound travels across these open expanses. Two guys want to kill us."

Truck traffic out almost to the horizon in the distance proved Diane's point on how far the road was. "I can't do this," Carol said. "Yes, you can. It's the last one." They limped along to the place Diane had indicated, climbed down and dog paddled across the slough, a small, quiet one, with algae the color of phosphorescent puce lining the banks. Diane noticed that Carol tried to hold her breath the whole way. Carol gasped for air, gulped and held her breath again. "Just breathe normally," Diane told her.

"I can't. It stinks."

They reached the opposite bank, flicked off the spongy strings of algae that clung to their wet bodies and slowly worked their way up the cultivated ice plant, crushing it, as they climbed.

Carol tore open the plastic bag Diane had detached from her back, the Safeway sack that had served them so well. The contents fell to the dirt. They dressed quickly in their wet, rumpled clothes. Carol had a navy dress and Diane a black skirt and blouse with tiny white markings, dyed permanently red brown from the water and soil. Her black jacket was gone. Carol's navy one was still among their possessions, as was her large, silk, navy and gold scarf, crumpled in one of the pockets.

"You had better wear this, Diane," said Carol, making a triangle with the scarf and tying it around Diane's head. "Pull it on to cover your face if we have to talk to anyone. Your face is too battered. It may scare people who might otherwise help us. Your skin is hot. You feel okay?"

"I'll be fine."

Already the July air was heating up. They reached the narrow, county road and started back toward the entrance to the marina parking lot. Way in the distance behind them came the sound of an automobile engine. They increased their pace but it only intensified Carol's painful limp, so they resumed their original walking and tried to appear casual. The entrance to the marina was only sixty feet ahead when the small pickup truck with a tiny aluminum boat on top, slowed and passed them. It stopped opposite the gravel road leading into the marina. Two men in the cab conversed. On the passenger side, a man tossed out an empty whiskey pint bottle. The truck lurched into reverse and backed towards the approaching walkers. The driver stuck his head out the window and called back to the women.

"Excuse me, is there a launch ramp here?"

He pointed into the unpretentious complex of trailers and small buildings. Since there was a Lazy M Marina sign nailed to the fence post at the entrance, Diane decided the man must be illiterate or really drunk. Carol had stepped forward and slightly in front of Diane who clutched at the scarf so that only her good eye was visible. Carol hesitated.

"Yes," Diane said from behind the scarf.

"Yes, there is," repeated Carol, louder. "Right in there."

She waved her arm in the general direction of the compound, deliberately unspecific.

"Thanks. Something wrong with your friend?"

"Could you give us a lift to the sheriff's office?"

"Sorry, but we're going fishin'. I don't even know where the closest sheriff's office is. Go on over to those buildings. There's got to be a phone there somewhere." The driver shoved his truck in gear and drove toward the dusty, gravel road leading to the parking lot.

"Nice helpful types," Carol said, trying to wave the truck's dust away. "May they catch a turd-eating fish."

They were smiling when they walked through the entrance. Diane noticed a cafe in a trailer that had not been there twenty years ago. There were several large storage containers and a couple more mobile homes, which didn't look occupied, but everything else seemed preserved exactly as she had remembered it. The cafe wasn't open. Probably too early. They would have a phone. Then they saw it — a black van parked behind one of the mobile homes, just the back corner protruding.

"Diane —."

"This way, quick."

Diane turned to the left and headed for the cluster of small frame buildings. The closest one had a prominent Women sign on it. The old wood siding was painted yellow with white trim on the window frame.

"It's really been fixed up since I was here. Better than I remember it, fortunately," Diane said.

"Better?"

There was a cement walk. Cement steps replaced the old open wooden ones Diane remembered. The one room building was painted. The inside now had a modesty panel opposite the door. There were two sinks in a Formica counter, even a mirror. Diane saw herself and paused to touch her battered, bluish purple face and quickly turned away. Carol stared at herself in momentary shock and turned away, too. The windows were the same. A board replaced the absent pane of the lower part of one. The other had a thin, scratched coat of white paint on the glass.

"At least someone donated some soap to the cause," Carol said, seeing the used bar of blue soap on the sink. She turned on the faucet, which groaned and spat three angry bursts of rusty water into the sink before running clear. Carol whirled around, looked at Diane with narrowed eyes. "River water?"

"No. Let it run."

Carol began to wash very tentatively. "We've got to get tetanus shots right away," she said.

The crunching sound of tires on gravel moved past them, beyond the buildings to the ramp. It was the sound of a car and boat trailer swinging around to make ready for launch.

"What now?" Carol asked. "How can we get to the phone with those men here?"

Peeking cautiously through the upper portion of the painted window, Diane said, "The phone's out of order."

Carol, face dripping, hobbled over to see where Diane pointed. "The receiver's gone."

Diane brushed past the telephone problem and said, "One of us will have to keep watch from over there, somewhere in the shadows between all these little buildings. Maybe there's another bathroom in the cafe so people won't be using this one. Anyway, those men would never expect us here. We've come too far."

"Then why is the van here? Why's the phone broken? They're waiting for us! They're going to kill us!"

# Chapter 16

In the morning Evert Johns strode into Roger's room, pushing a wheelchair and trailing a huge male nurse. "I've come to take you home, Roger. You're signed out. Doctor says you can travel, provided we don't bump you around too much."

"Huh? Evert? What — "

"They paged me at the airport. I turned right around and came back last night. Early this morning, actually. You were out of it.

"The FBI nailed Shade, by the way. About to board a flight for Geneva. It sure helps that the Commerce Secretary was my college roommate. Shade almost made it. The FBI held up the boarding. Shade didn't take it very gracefully. Took a swing at one of the agents. They have a silencer, not the gun, but they're working on it. The silencer's probably enough."

"Shade shot me?" Roger's good hand made a motion toward his shoulder then gave up.

"Tried to kill you. Almost succeeded."

\* \* \*

In the delta the sound of crunching gravel came again — this time a vehicle parked close to the cafe. There were the sounds of early morning greetings. Someone walked from the ramp area

140

across to the cafe, unlocked the door and went inside. Carol and Diane listened intently to every sound, with the alertness of the hunted. The trailer housing the tiny restaurant was backed close to one side of the remodeled shack that was the Women's room. They could overhear anyone outside, near their building.

"Carol, you rest here. I'll try to keep watch on things out there, then we'll trade off. If I yell, you come running for dear life. In a place like this, people occasionally leave their cars running while they load their gear. If we can get a car, preferably, a car or a truck without a trailer attached, we could go to the authorities.

"Steal one?"

"Borrow, temporarily."

"Oh, geez, the van. What if those two shoot us in the parking lot when we try to get a car?"

"At least maybe there'll be witnesses. "

Carol slid to the floor in the corner where she would not be visible from the door. She leaned against the wall and waved her agreement. More tires crunched in the parking lot, at least two vehicles this time. Diane went out and found a narrow space between the snug configuration of buildings and trailers. By maneuvering through the warren of buildings and containers, she could observe the marina's staging and parking areas. Business was picking up.

A dark sports car whipped into the marina, sought out a remote parking spot and stopped. Adjusting his sunglasses and looking around, the tall, blond, young man checked his watch. He looked up to see an apparently familiar car with a boat in tow, turning into the parking lot. Hastily, gathering his gear and slalom ski with double boot bindings from the hatchback, he locked up and headed for the boat now parked in the make-ready area. The boat owner was an even taller young man with sandy hair, and the same lean build. A third young man with dark hair and muscular build was shorter than his two friends. Two more competition skis went into the boat. With quick, jovial greetings, the young men had the boat launched inside of five minutes.

When the car pulled the empty trailer in a wide arc closer to the buildings, to make room for another boat about to be launched, Diane saw the US Rowing decal on the rear side window. Rowers, of course, thought Diane. At least two of them were. The shorter man might have been a coxswain once, but he was too muscular now. Minutes after entering the parking lot, the boat headed out under the trestle.

The experience of being kidnapped and threatened had trampled Diane's confidence. Seeing herself in the mirror, looking like a police photograph of a battered woman had not helped. She struggled with the idea of approaching the young men for help, but they had launched before she could decide what to do. She jumped at each noise, imagining the kidnappers finding her crouched and stiff. In her mind she saw splatters of her blood on the dirty white wall where she hid, then her dark blood pumping from a slit artery in her neck and pooling in the dust.

Several more boats launched before things slowed to just an occasional customer at the cafe now and then. The black van was still in place, but Diane couldn't see it without sticking her head out into plain view. She didn't want to risk that. She went to check on Carol. No one had attempted to use the Women's room, but Carol had been frightened by a couple of men who went by to get to the Men's, another made-over shack next door.

The sight of the black van had taken reason from Carol and Diane. Not trusting that someone might assist them, the bedraggled women became increasingly fearful and jumpy.

"Carol?" Diane whispered when she came through the doorway.

"Anything yet?"

"No. Things have slowed way down. Maybe someone will get careless when they are pulling out at the end of the day. I think I'll stay here with you for a while. It's so hot."

She pulled the scarf from her head and sank onto the floor near Carol. "Look at your hand," Carol said. "You've got red streaks running up your hand!"

"It doesn't hurt too much. I feel sick, though. Wish it weren't so hot."

"You stay and rest. If a car comes, I'll go watch," Carol said.

Diane gave a single nod of assent and closed her eyes. Drawing up her knees, she folded her arms, and put her head down. She was damp with perspiration. The wall supported her back, but the sound of tires on gravel kept her mind from relaxing. Carol left. With the bright mid-morning sun, the temperature rose higher, pushing ninety. Carol returned. Diane realized that she must have dozed because she was not aware of Carol's presence until she whispered her name.

"Some boats have pulled out," Carol reported. "Fishermen. Those two drunk men we met on the road dropped their boat while they were trying to slide it on top of their truck. Can't believe you didn't hear the commotion. Everything's quiet now."

"There's no air in here"

The welts and scratches from the berry vines itched unmercifully. A trickle of perspiration ran down Diane's swollen face. Carol reached over, gently brushed it away.

"It's my hand that's throbbing. Your foot must be too. My face is sore, but it looks worse than it feels. I saw myself in the mirror," Diane said. "It's —."

The building shuddered. An explosion! Shock and sound waves from a distance, rumbled by them. Diane shot to her feet and went out the door, concentrating on the sound. Carol was completely confused. Diane stood on a mound of dirt, completely out in the open, staring at the sky toward the east. Another secondary explosion, like a muffled gunshot was barely discernible, noticeable only because of the stillness of the hour.

"What is it?" Carol whispered, timidly joining Diane.

They couldn't see anything in the direction they were watching, beyond the big mobile home up on the levee, perpendicular to the launch ramp. Diane watched the sky. Carol followed her gaze. Nothing. She was hot — feverish. Her foot screaming in complaint with each step, she turned to her friend.

"Diane, What's the matter? What is it?"

Diane did not answer. She glanced at Carol, then back at the sky. It was an odd glance, blank and yet not blank, the look of intense thought or of confusion, or preoccupation. Then Diane pointed. Carol turned and saw a thin column of black smoke undulating lazily straight up into the quiet blue. As they watched, the column began drifting westward.

"What is it?" Carol repeated, now referring to the smoke.

"An explosion of some kind, I guess. Let's get back inside."

Diane returned to the Women's room. Carol spent another pensive moment, observing the smoke, then she turned slowly and joined Diane inside.

"Carol."

"What?"

"You need to know something."

"Okay, shoot."

"When I was little, playing on Guam with my brothers, we found a Japanese machine gun bunker left over from the war. It was at one end of the officers' beach."

"Guam?" Carol scratched her head and frowned.

"Yeah, I lived there in nineteen fifty-one and fifty-two. The bunker was dome shaped with a real thick ceiling, muggy, dim, smelly from rotting vegetation inside." Diane's voice sounded like she was narrating a movie. She seemed to be nine, inside the bunker again. "It was built on a finger of black lava that jutted out into the ocean at one end of the beach. All overgrown and surrounded by jungle. We frightened a young Monitor lizard, about two and half feet long. It flicked its forked tongue at us and disappeared out the long, rectangular gun slot. When I approached the slot and looked out, I was surprised. And shocked."

Diane turned to Carol, her voice back to normal. "The image jolted me. I've never forgotten it. From the darkness of the bunker, I looked out at the glaring, brightness of the whole lagoon. The wild beauty, vivid turquoises, blues, greens and browns leaped at me. Yet, I knew that a single machine gun could kill anyone out there. Nine years old and I knew that.

"When I walked back to the beach, I turned, looked for the bunker. I couldn't see it, not even a hint of where it might be. No one coming from the sea could have survived to get to where I was standing."

"Diane, why are you telling me? It's interesting, but..."

"Because I was back there again, outside, just a while ago, before the explosion. Hiding in the shadows, squinting at that bright parking lot, I suddenly smelled the jungle growth and sea spray, saw the colors, everything, all over again. And, and, oh, God, because I needed to tell you."

Diane didn't go on. Carol let it be. A boat could be heard pulling slowly up to the dock. Soon a car engine in the parking lot alerted them someone else was pulling out for the day. Diane went to watch, scarf back in place.

The three young men who had gone out for an early morning ski were back. They took a little longer to pull their boat out than they did to launch, but they were still fast. They wiped down the hull and stowed their gear. The car with the trailer was left unattended when they went into the cafe, but Diane had seen the driver jangle the keys as he walked inside. Even if the keys had been left in the car, a clean getaway pulling a boat would be impossible. There was the matter of the third guy with his fast sports car, too. The young men emerged before she could think further, said their good-byes and went to their cars. Each carried a green can of soda. Diane licked her lips. There was the water faucet in the Women's room, but neither she nor Carol had drunk more than a few handfuls.

Pulling out of the driveway onto the road, the car with the boat had to brake abruptly for a speeding jalopy of a pickup truck. The once white truck swung wide around the front of the car and, wheels spinning on the loose rocks, raced into the marina and up to where stairs led to the big trailer on the levee.

"Carol," Diane yelled amid the commotion. "Carol!"

The situation held promise. The car and boat pulled fully out onto the road and drove off. The old truck had sped right by the chocolate brown Porsche 944, close enough to touch, completely engulfing it in dust. Diane thought she could see the sports car driver's lips moving, but maybe she imagined it. After several moments the driver started again. He turned onto the road and headed after his friends.

Carol stood at Diane's shoulder. Diane led the way back, along the other aisle, to view the ramp. The truck driver honked his horn and was pushing and banging on his door to get out. The old gentleman who collected the launch fees shuffled towards him.

"What's the rush?" he called to the man climbing free of his truck. He left the motor running, the cantankerous door flung wide open.

"Boat blew up! One of those ski jobs. Couple of my field hands came running to me with the news. Probably killed someone. Reckon I better call the sheriff. You see it? Hear the explosion?"

"Heard the explosion. Thought it was dynamite blastin' somewhere. Saw the smoke, though. See that little smudge in the sky. That's where it was."

"Well, can I use your phone?"

"Sure. Come on inside."

The old man led the way laboriously up the steps to the mobile home atop the levee.

The TV blared because his wife refused to wear a hearing aid. When the men entered, she warned them with a finger to her lips, waved and pointed at the set. The men went around the counter to the phone in the kitchen area. Neither saw or heard anything happening in the parking lot.

"Ever drive an old truck?" Diane asked.

"I can learn," Carol answered.

"No, I'll drive. It didn't look quite this bad, but we used to have a sixty-five Chevy truck. Let's go."

Diane and Carol scampered across the short distance to the truck. Carol, adrenalin pumping, ignored her foot, which had started to bleed again. She slid into the open door on the driver's side then across the seat to the passenger's side. Diane jumped in right behind her, tugging violently at the door to get it closed. She jammed the engine into reverse, plowed backward all the way across the parking lot before stopping to grind the motor into first and swing the truck toward the gate.

"Diane," Carol yelled, "The van— that black van. It's not the same one. I think this one's newer."

"What?"

"Too late now. Forget it. We're outta here."

They felt good to be moving again, moving fast. By the time the dust settled in the parking lot, the rickety truck was disappearing far down the road. The motor was obviously struggling, so Diane backed off a bit. She slowed when they approached the stop sign for the two-lane highway ahead. The intersection was a ninety degree turn. Diane went onto the shoulder, almost going in the ditch, taking her left turn at nearly fifty miles per hour.

Cautiously Carol suggested, "Shouldn't we be going the other way — Uh, Mount Diablo and all?"

"That only applied to the water or open country, not to the roads. We're on Clifton Court. I'm taking us to Altamont Pass. We have to backtrack a little. This is Tomato Curve coming up."

They took a sweeping curve with just the slightest reduction in speed.

"Tomato Curve?"

"We named it for the tomato truck that overturned there one year."

Carol imagined smashed tomatoes, like blood, splattered across the highway. They roared on, ignoring the fifty miles per hour sign, racing past the massive pumping station that pulls the water from Clifton Court Forebay into the huge California Aqueduct and the Delta-Mendota canal. Approaching a green Alameda County sign, Diane began pumping the brakes. Another ninety degree turn appeared, to the right this time. They swerved through it on the shoulder, spraying gravel and dirt, and sped up again.

"What road is this?" asked Carol, seeing no sign.

"Mountain House. I know it by the county sign."

Carol began to think about her husband, Roger, and wondered why the kidnappers wanted him. She opened the glove compartment and found a handgun.

"Look at this." She said. "It may come in handy." Rummaging further she found a box of pellets. "Guess it's just a pellet gun. Sure looks real."

"A deliberate look alike, probably."

They overtook and passed a tractor creeping along at seven miles an hour. It was a blind pass over a little rise. In the rearview mirror Diane could see the farmer waving both fists in the air.

"Been over this road before, haven't you? Lucky no one was coming," Carol said. "Wonder if he's the yokel who shot at us."

"It's been years. Damn!"

"What?"

"We're out of gas — according to this gauge, anyway."

"Oh, shoot. There's nothing much around here. How far to the freeway?"

"Not too far."

Carol saw the little Mountain House School and the twenty miles per hour speed zone sign. "Must be a school," she said to encourage Diane to slow down. The chained, fenced play yard and drawn window shades held no promise. Closed for the summer. The truck leapt along, bouncing and complaining like it would fly apart whenever it went over a bump and crashed back to the pavement.

Diane finally began to slow when the road curved more abruptly. She actually slowed way down around a blind turn and across a little bridge. Carol could see a stop sign ahead. Then she realized that the road ended. They would have to go right or left.

"Grant Line Road," Diane announced. "And there's our ride!"

The dusty Porsche from the marina was pulled up to an old public phone booth. The sign on the roof of a rundown, clapboard building announced, Mountain House Road Bar. Carol surveyed the array of Harleys in front of the bar.

A biker watched the rusty, white wreck of a truck run the stop sign, and speed into the parking lot. It barreled up to the phone booth and stopped in a mammoth cloud of dust. He watched someone get out on the passenger side and the truck roar over to the far side of the building and again skid to a stop. The biker started yelling obscenities at them for raising so much dust.

Diane gave the door a hard push, but when it did not open, she slid across the seat and out the passenger side. Carol confronted the young man in the phone booth.

"Please call the Highway Patrol for me at once."

"Lady, the phone ate all my change, I'm in a hurry, and the phone's not working."

"We need your help. We will not hurt you, but you must help us."

The young man shook his head and opened his mouth to protest when Carol raised the gun from the fold in her skirt. Mouth still open, he stared at the gun.

"Hang up the telephone." Carol said. "We need you to drive us to Danville or to the first Highway Patrol, or sheriff we meet. What's your name, young man?"

"Jeff. I'm Jeff." He hung up. Something about this woman reminded the young man of his mother. It was crazy, he knew. What was it?

"This nice gentleman has agreed to help us," Carol announced to Diane.

"Great. I'll ride in back."

"Whoa. What are you doing? You can dial 911, or something, from the bar. I don't have time for this."

Diane countered, "We don't know where the men who kidnapped us are right now. What if they don't have 911 out here? We look like hell, have no money, and that bozo is mad at us." She gestured towards the red-faced biker. "Get in the car, kid. This is an emergency."

"Danville, huh?" Jeff asked, surprised at himself.

"Yes, or the first police officer you see. Drive as fast as you like. We'll be in your debt forever."

The tires sprayed gravel and dust leaving the parking lot.

"Put the gun away. It's dangerous. I'll help you without it. I'm late, anyway. Might as well take the rest of the day off."

"We're really sorry for all the trouble we're causing you, but we didn't have any other choice," said Carol. "We think this is just a pellet gun, but it could put your eye out."

"Real fine, car-jacked by two women with a pellet gun. Real fine." He sighed heavily, a smile playing across his lips. It was too strange. "Well, we need to get you safely into the hands of the authorities. Promise me that you'll fill me in on the full story when it's all over."

They were doing ninety-five as the Porsche swung right and went up the grade merging onto Highway 580. It hit ninety-six to a hundred until they were over the amber hills of the summit at Altamont Pass, then they raced down into the shimmering heat waves rising from the Livermore Valley. From what passed for a back seat, Diane stopped watching the speedometer which was now flirting with one hundred ten.

They saw a patrol car coming up the hill on the opposite side. They slowed and started darting around cars, weaving in and out of the lanes, but the officer must have been watching only cars going in his direction. Then, too late to stop, and from the fast lane, they saw another patrol car. It was parked by the weigh station with no one in it. Too late, Jeff slowed. "Sure hard to attract these guys when you want to," he said.

"He must be inside," Carol said. "We could pull over and drive back on the shoulder."

Looking back, Diane caught sight of a dark van coming up on them fast. It must have been going one hundred fifteen or more.

Panic stricken, she squeaked, "Black van! Black van behind us," and ducked down.

Carol swung around and sank below her seat back in a single motion. That was all it took to see the van overtaking them, the driver's face obscured by a dark baseball cap. The van was the same model she remembered. Jeff pushed the Porsche faster.

"What's the deal with a black van? He doesn't seem to be paying any particular attention to us."

"We were kidnapped by two men with a black van. They took us to an old houseboat that was barely floating. Left us there tied up. We escaped. Where is he?"

"Right behind us. Stay down."

He moved out of the van's way, not just over one lane, but two. The van took no notice. It continued barreling down the fast lane nearly driving over cars too slow moving out of its way.

"The Danville turnoff is coming up. You can sit up now. The van is by us. He's going straight."

"This is car One Niner. I've just picked up the mahogany Porsche. It exited and is proceeding north on 680 toward Danville/Walnut Creek. I can provide backup but I'm headed east beyond the turnoff. I'm proceeding to the Hopyard Road exit and will circle back. Seventeen should see him soon. The black Dodge van Eighteen called in is headed for Oakland. Got anyone ready on down the road? He was doing ninety-seven to a hundred on my radar. I clocked the Porsche at ninety. Where do you want the backup?"

"Roger, Nineteen. Proceed west on 580 to backup car Twenty-three. She's at the Livermore/Pleasanton exit and should have the van any second. We have Seventeen and Six waiting to bracket the Porsche. Shucks, we've even got one of the County Sheriff's boys in the area investigating a suspicious box of toxics along the roadside. Twenty-three said she thought it was Deputy McClatchy."

"Roger that. I'm exiting to return westbound on 580 to backup Twenty-three with the van."

The CHP officer slowed for the stop at the exit, circled back in the direction he had come, and turned on his flashing lights.

151

Carol and Diane noticed the increase in traffic on 680 and thought it a little strange. Jeff moved into the fast lane and began passing the slower cars. From four lanes away they saw the empty sheriff's car, too late to stop.

"Should I get over to the shoulder and stop? We could hike back to him."

"No, we're past him and City Hall isn't too much further," Carol said.

"That a patrol car ahead?" Jeff was working his way to the slow lane.

"Where?" asked Carol.

"Way up there on the side of the road."

"I've picked up the Porsche. He's slowed way down and moved into the slow lane. I'm sure he has seen me so I'll move out and force him to go around me. There are so many of us out here, we have the traffic all but stopped."

"Roger, Six. Let me know when you have everything under control."

Closer now, they knew it was definitely a patrol car. The traffic was moving about fifty-two in their lane. Switching on his turn signal, the driver of the Porsche pulled off the same moment the patrol car pulled on. The young man jumped from the car, waving his arms in the air.

The patrolman hit his flashers, drove back onto the shoulder, screeched to a stop and jerked into reverse. In a trail of dust that nearly caused several accidents among the passersby, he backed his cruiser toward the Porsche at forty miles per hour.

"I think he sees us," Jeff said.

"Just stay where you are until I tell you to move," the voice gun boomed at him when the cruiser stopped. "Do not move."

Carol tucked the pellet gun under her seat.

"Emergency! Emergency!" Jeff yelled to no avail.

He kept his hands on the top of the car in the patrolman's view and did as he was told. The officer was involved in conversation on his radio.

"I'm glad no one's having a baby. This is taking forever."

The cruiser's door opened.

"Officer, this is an emergency. We need your assistance immediately. I've got two kidnap victims here."

The officer pulled out his ticket book and leaned over to survey the passengers and instantly recognized the traumatized expressions and physical abuse. The kid was talking; the woman pressed against the back seat demanded to see his identification, and words came in a non-stop torrent from the woman in the front.

"You've got to help us. Kidnappers are after my husband. We're in danger. They'll kill him — kill us. We took the truck with the gun in the glove compartment — just a pellet gun."

"Easy, easy," he said softly. "I'm with the California Highway Patrol." His left hand indicated his nameplate, Baker. "You're safe. Stay calm. I can't help you unless you stay calm." To the driver he asked, "Is there a gun?"

"Yeah, they used it to force me to drive them to Danville. It looks real, but it's probably a pellet gun because they found a box of pellets with it in the truck they stole.

"They stole a truck?"

"They told me this while we were driving. They are very frightened. I feel sorry for them."

Carol continued, "There was a black van in the driveway. My dog, Whiskers, ran away. Please warn Roger. A black van just passed us, on the freeway, just a few minutes ago."

"Who has the gun?"

"The one in front."

Patrolman Baker leveled his gun at the car. Into his shoulder radio, he called for back up. "It's more complicated than we first thought: possible weapon, possible kidnappings, kidnapping victims. Contact the Sheriff's Department. I passed a deputy's car just a mile or two back. Have him get up here — fast!"

The sight of his gun trained on them did not have a calming effect. Carol, in front, talked faster, louder.

"Lady, lady, I want you to move your right hand very slowly to the door handle.

"I don't know why they want to kidnap him."

"Lady! Pipe down and listen to me. I'm here to help you. Put your right hand on the door handle. Your left hand on the dash. Do it! You in the back, don't move a muscle!"

Carol tried to turn her attention to the door handle. She didn't find it instantly, but she stopped talking. At last, she put her left hand on the dashboard and the fingers of her right hand found the door latch.

"That's great. Now slowly open the door. That's it. Push it all the way open. Now very slowly, step out of the car."

"I'm afraid. What about Diane? What if that black van comes back?"

"It's okay. I've called for backup. You're going to be okay. You're safe. We need to get you both out of the car so we can find out what happened and how we can help."

Baker's calm voice communicated confidence, his tone battling her hysteria. Slowly she lifted her feet out onto the ground and he noticed the tortured bare feet, the makeshift bandage. With her two hands on the top of the door, she pulled herself up and stood outside the car, hesitated a moment and took a step away. She did not appear to have a weapon.

"Move back. Put your hands up on the top of the car. I mean it! Do not make any other move."

"Go around and help the other one out, real slow," Officer Baker told Jeff.

"He's going to help you out," Baker said to Diane. "Move slowly."

Diane was wedged in sideways, knees bent and feet up on the other tiny indention called a seat. Baker saw the puffy, bruised face, the cuts and scratches, the bare feet. She could not have moved from that seat quickly, under any circumstances. The young man pulled the front seat forward and offered a hand

154

to Diane struggling to get out. A Contra Costa County sheriff's car approached in the slow lane, parked on the shoulder behind them.

Deputy McClatchy stepped out of his car. "Ms. Steadhold?"

"Possible weapon in the vehicle, Deputy," said the CHP officer.

"But I can positively ID that woman. She's Carol Steadhold, the mayor of Danville. What the hell happened?"

"We were kidnapped yesterday. They meant to get Roger — I don't know why. But he's in New York and they took us. We surprised them at the house."

"The car, your car is still at your house. I was there, but nothing seemed to be wrong, just a bit odd. I questioned your gardener about the front door being open. Planned to question him again, if I didn't hear from you today. Is he involved?"

Carol did not hear him, so intent was she to get her story out. Her hands began moving, animating her words. "They were going to kill us. Thank God, Diane got us through the delta."

"Where's the gun, ma'am?" The CHP Officer Baker asked Carol.

"Under the seat, in front."

"Are there any other weapons? Do any of you have a weapon on you?"

"Only the gun. We found it in the truck. It was in the glove compartment."

"Truck?" Deputy McClatchy's expression changed.

"The truck we stole at the marina," Carol said.

"You have the right to remain silent," began the Officer Baker.

"Would that be a white, sixty-three Chevy pick-up from Lazy M Marina?" Deputy Sheriff McClatchy asked. The call for assistance from the CHP had come right on top of the Contra Costa County Sheriff's report of the stolen truck.

"You have the right to an attorney." No one was listening to the increasingly frustrated Officer Baker. "Anything you say may be used against you in a court of law."

"We left it at that bar place at Mountain House Road. That's where we persuaded this nice young man to help us."

"Interesting word, <u>persuaded</u>," said Jeff with a laugh.

"We had to escape," Carol said to McClatchy. "They wanted my husband, Roger. We must get word to him. Can we notify the FBI? Those men are around somewhere, but I've no idea who wanted Roger kidnapped or why."

Diane said, "We're certain that they were working for someone else. They were upset about how that person would react. They planned to kill us. We had to escape."

The CHP Officer Baker finished reciting their rights to them, but no one noticed. He double-checked with McClatchy. "I'll follow you to Danville and sign off. It's all yours. If you need me, you know how to get in touch." To Jeff, he said, "I'll forget the speeding. I'd done it too, with that cargo." He indicated Diane and Carol with his thumb. "You're going to be busy. We'll need a statement. All that goes with it. This kind of thing sure generates the paperwork."

*   *   *

Early that morning, in the motel in Livermore, Jimmy Thrasher looked at the framed print of a mountain scene on the wall. He had spent a sleepless night. He worried about Rudy, about what he would do to the women when they went back to the houseboat, but he had given up on trying to suggest anything else. Rudy, snoring, gave him a creepy, unpleasant feeling.

The same thoughts swirled in his mind as he chewed his dirty, fingernails. Should I try to call Adenhauer again? I'm just a car thief. How did I get mixed up in this? Kidnapping and this shit. Rudy tossed around during the night too. Something's bothering him. What is it with the ski boat? Rudy wants to sell it. A few thousand bucks. So what? Who am I kidding? It'd be a few thousand more than he has now. Probably has no thought of splitting it with me, neither.

By nine o'clock both men were awake and dressing. They drank a cup of instant coffee in their motel room and headed for the car. They didn't speak much. Jimmy fidgeted, miserable with apprehension, Rudy sullen and silent.

Jimmy drove. It was his car. At least it was his now. Rudy seemed to relax. The muscles in his face and jaw returned to normal, so Jimmy tried some conversation.

"There's no rush, Rudy. Let's drive on to Tracy and get that big breakfast we talked about last night."

Rudy said, "Either that or we could have a meal in Stockton after we stop at the houseboat, so I can drive the ski boat up there. Meet at the consignment yard, like we said last night."

Encouraged by Rudy's unusual ambivalence and his actually giving him a choice, Jimmy chose breakfast although he was not hungry. It would buy a little more time and it might keep Rudy in a better mood.

"Yeah, Jimmy. You're entitled to a good breakfast."

They drove to the outskirts of Tracy and searched out a place that suited Rudy. He rejected the first two possibilities before agreeing to the third.

They went into the restaurant and sat at a booth. The service was slow. When breakfast arrived, Rudy's robust appetite surprised Jimmy, who had trouble getting the greasy food down.

Finally, the ordeal was over and they headed out of Tracy for Grant Line Road and the delta, finding their way after a couple of wrong turns and some backtracking. They were not used to going in from that direction. Jimmy became increasingly apprehensive the closer they came to the houseboat. Approaching the houseboat, Rudy, too, became agitated. "Hold it! What was that?"

"What?"

"Stop. Back up. No, stop the car."

Jimmy obeyed. Rudy leaped from the car and returned, his face distorted in rage. He threw a woman's shoe, hard at Jimmy through the open car door and walked on several more steps, bent over and picked up something. This shoe he bounced off the car's windshield in front of Jimmy's face.

"Shoes? Rudy?"

But a thought was dawning on Jimmy's poor brain.

"You moron! The women! They got away! You let them get away!"

"They were tied up! Just like when you left. I didn't change a thing!"

Jimmy was getting hot too. He had enough. Rudy got back into the car, his jaw set, his mood infecting the air around him.

"Drive on up to the dock. Let's see what we find."

Rudy picked up the shoe wedged in the planking of the dock and threw it over the side. The sliding glass door to the houseboat was open, so was the back door. They saw the smeared bloody fingerprints in the galley, on the doors, smudges everywhere. They moved toward the stern and found the ropes that had bound the women. Jimmy bent down and examined the old, frayed line that he'd used to tie Diane's hands. It was intact, untied, not cut. His back to Rudy, the hairs on the back of his neck prickled. He sensed more than heard the safety go off. That moment he realized everything. He knew what had happened to Manny, years ago. Why hadn't he believed the rumors? And the others — Rudy must have done them too. The women had escaped, but that didn't even matter. Rudy had planned this from the start. Jimmy didn't turn around. His eyes darted out the back to the brown water, the green foliage beyond and the bright sunshine. The floor's ugly, rust colored linoleum slapped his face.

The first shot went through his left lung the second through the back of his head.

"Stupid fuckup."

In the instant after the shots, the sound waves reverberating, two striking yellow eyes, flecked with dark gray, blinked. The Great Blue Heron lifted from her perch and flew in a powerful glide along the water, silently, swiftly. She gained altitude at the mouth of the slough and disappeared heading west towards Mount Diablo, higher and higher.

Rudy took the wallet from Jimmy's back jeans pocket. He kicked at the body to move it enough to step past. He returned to the car, grabbed his duffel bag, thought about trying to wipe away his fingerprints, but decided not to bother and went back aboard. He would leave the state before anyone would know who did it. Pulling the front sliding door closed and the ratty curtain across, he then strode by Jimmy's bleeding head, through the back door and untied the ski boat. He tossed his bag into the observer's seat, climbed in and pushed off. Leaning over the side and with a cupped hand he brought in some water to wipe off the dried blood droplets and smears Diane had left behind. The boat drifted.

Those stupid women had tried to escape in his boat. He became obsessed with getting the blood wiped off. He took out a kerchief, wet it and wiped down the interior. The boat drifted farther and farther out toward the mouth to the next slough, propelled by Rudy's movements and the light morning breeze.

Finally, satisfied, he pulled out his keys, found the one for the boat and sat down heavily in the driver's seat. He pumped the gas vigorously, excessively working the hand throttle, his annoyance getting the better of him. He lit a cigarette to relax and think, but he was anxious not to waste any more time. He gave the throttle two more pumps for extra insurance, and cranked the engine with the key. The engine cover's image, splitting open on a fiery red and yellow hell, flashed in the large ski mirror the same instant it shattered, but it had no time to register on his brain.

The swirling gasoline fumes trapped inside the engine cover ignited with an explosion that could be heard for more than six miles down wind. Burning fragments floated softly down, raining over a wide area. Rudy died instantly.

# Chapter 17

Jake Hartig ambled into Canby International at nine-fifty, carrying on a conversation with himself and frightening those he passed, except the receptionist and security people, who already thought he was odd. He found his way to his office where he alarmed Alice, his secretary, by using his briefcase to brush everything but her computer from her desk to the floor. Alice telephoned downstairs at once.

"Security."

"I've got a man out of control up here. It's Jake Hartig in Personnel. I need help right away."

"Sure thing. What's he doing?"

"He knocked all my work off my desk. No word, simply swept my desk clean. He's in his office talking like he's several different people. He's throwing files at the ceiling, emptying whole drawers. I think it's a complete breakdown. Hurry!"

The security man hung up and rushed to the office. "Rosie, take the front desk. Call the police. Emergency on the twentieth floor. That dork from Personnel. He's flipped. Robert, Umberto, come with me. Bring a net."

"Wish we had one. What's the guy doing?"

"Making a mess, throwing files around, talking to people who ain't there."

Jake had begun removing his clothes and was nude when security came for him. He scratched his body, his head, said he itched all over. The police took him to Highland Hospital for observation, an involuntary seventy-two hour hold.

The media picked up parts of the story while Roger slept fitfully in the company jet, and Evert worked on damage control. Evert telephoned Taipei, tracked down Hsing Tom and spent a half-hour talking with him. A call came in from Oakland headquarters to let Evert know about Jake Hartig's being hauled off for observation. Another call from headquarters, the market was reacting to rumors of the arrest of Canby's chief financial officer and the possible embezzlement of company funds.

"What next?" Evert asked aloud. "I need some positives."

Roger stirred and mumbled Carol's name. Evert heard and said, "Of course, I'll call her right now. Couldn't reach her last night." He grabbed the telephone again and asked Janet to get a hold of Carol Steadhold. "Put her through as soon as you reach her." When the call finally came back, it was not Carol, but Janet. "Carol Steadhold is in the emergency room having a foot stitched up and receiving treatment for shock, cuts and bruises."

"What? What happened?"

"Two of them, Carol and another woman, were kidnapped yesterday!" Janet's voice reflected how incredulous the news seemed. "They're both okay now, pretty beaten up. I told the doctor that Carol's husband had been shot, but he was recovering, and that he was flying home. The doctor said Carol's desperate to talk to him. She'll be able to come to the phone in about ten minutes."

"Put her right through, when her call comes. I'll wake Roger and explain what I can."

When Roger and Carol appeared to be winding down their private conversation, Evert intervened and put on the speakerphone. "The media is having a field day, Carol, as you can imagine. I need a positive face on this situation. Let's brainstorm a few minutes."

In Oakland, late that afternoon, each department head at Canby headquarters announced to their sections that all employees were requested to attend a closed meeting in the auditorium at three the next afternoon, prior to a formal press conference at four thirty. Informally, department heads could say that the meeting was not about a layoff, merger, buy out or financial collapse. Canby was robust. The employees worried nonetheless. Speculation fired like static charges among the cubicles.

Shortly after four the next day, security people in the white marble and reflective chrome lobby kept the early reporters and camera people well back from the double-door entries to Canby's auditorium, lest the media forgot they were invited guests on private property. When finally the smiling employees streamed out, the reporters shouted questions and surged. No one answered the shouts, but there were smiles and some thumbs-up signs. The auditorium emptied and the media, intrigued and suspicious at the same time, filed into the room. The camera people poured into the open space in front of the stage. Reporters jostled each other for the closest rows of seats. Some employees, unable to resist the show, returned and sat in the back to watch.

Off stage, Carol could hear the noisy buzz of the big room. Like hunting hounds with the scent, she thought. She leaned down and squeezed the fingers protruding from Roger's cast too tightly. He winced. "Oops, sorry," she said, and patted his good arm. She could see the five armless leather chairs on stage, to one side of the podium. Evert Johns came up to them, nodded and headed into the lights. The sound of his shoes striding across the stage silenced the auditorium and charged the air. Carol listened while he welcomed the media, explained the ground rules and promised to answer all questions at the end of his announcement. He read his statement and then introduced Hsing Tom and Shona Oliver. Tsing walked across the stage looking surprising refreshed for having made a thirteen-hour flight from Taiwan. Carol knew she looked like hell. She glanced at Diane.

The bruises around Diane's eyes and nose had darkened, looking worse than ever. "I appreciate your being here, Diane. I really mean it."

Diane smiled her swollen smile. "Bed, breakfast, unlimited phone calls. How could I say 'no'?"

On stage, Evert commended Hsing for his diligence and recognized him and his chief accountant, Shona Oliver, for being the first people to spot the financial irregularities. Spontaneous applause burst from the employees in the rear of the auditorium. The employees rose to their feet. It set the pattern for the introductions to follow.

Next Carol heard Evert say, "Carol Steadhold and Diane Lind." She clasped Diane's good hand and the two or them, bruised and bandaged, hobbled across the stage. Carol waved to the audience. Evert leaned in to whisper encouragement to each of them, Carol waved again, and they moved to stand by their chairs as Roger was rolled across the stage in a wheelchair, his shoulder and arm encased in the awkward plaster cast designed to keep his clavicle immobile. The employees in the back were on their feet applauding. Evert introduced Roger Steadhold to the press and explained his condition.

Last, Evert Johns introduced the man pushing the wheelchair, Al Gonzales, Canby's newest employee. He was the man who had prevented Roger's briefcase from being stolen, the briefcase containing Hsing Tom's note and the financial data. Evert told each person's story as he or she was introduced. Things were going well. Positive. Under control. Perfect, thought Carol. Then the questions began.

"Mr. Johns, how do you explain the gap in time between Mr. Tom's finding the problems: your own chief financial officer embezzling something like one and a half million dollars, and today, when Canby is finally taking corrective action?"

"I take complete responsibility, myself."

"Mr. Johns, Are you planning to resign? If not, don't you think your stockholders have the right to replace you for the mishandling of this situation?"

"The stockholders have a right to a full and complete explanation. I will abide by their judgement."

It's publicity that counts, Carol reminded herself. Good is best, but mixed, or even certain bad publicity didn't hurt, not for name recognition.

And, the media became fascinated with the story: Shade Nettle's arrest, his embezzlement of what was looking more like two million from Canby, the negotiations with the two Swiss banks Nettle seemed to favor, the kidnapping of Diane and herself and the violent deaths of the kidnappers.

The San Jose Mercury News, the major paper in Diane's area, interviewed the two women the day after the press conference in Oakland. "I wouldn't have gone into that water, if it hadn't been for Diane. She saved my life," Carol told them. The reporter speculated about how the ski boat might have blown up, but the women provided no help there.

Other Bay Area news agencies picked up the story of the women's escape. Summer can be a slow news time, Diane remembered. But the story was really about Canby and Carol and Roger.

Within the week, the Oakland police working with the FBI, found Jake Hartig's second phone number, an unlisted one, in Jimmy Thrasher's apartment. Written on the wall, by the phone in Rudy Silva's place, they found the name Adenhauer and the same unlisted number. The photograph of the Nettles and the Steadholds that Carol had hidden on the houseboat came from a roll that included an additional picture found in Rudy's trash.

Carol, gearing for the Congressional election a year and a half away, knew she needed to keep her name before the public. As time passed, she mentioned Diane less in her television and talk show appearances. Diane had all the recognition she needed. No one challenged her reelection bid that fall, which saved her from the heavy campaigning. Carol became a high-profile member of a victims rights organization. She championed environmental efforts to clean up the delta's water and joined those who wanted to slow the contracted water allotments to southern California.

.

# Chapter 18

## July 1994

Shade Nettle's attorney explained that the prosecutor had motive. Also, everyone at the departure gate at Kennedy had witnessed his resisting arrest. Furthermore, one of the valet parking attendants at the Biltmore had positively identified Nettle as the man to whom he had talked the evening Roger was shot. The attorney warned Nettle that the prosecutor would try to goad him. The deputy district attorney was a good-looking woman, in a brassy, hard way. Shirley Frost graduated number four in her law school class at Yale, and she made her name in the New York DA's office. She had not done it by being nice. Nettle's attorney urged him to stay calm and quiet in their meeting, but the deputy district attorney had a needling, self-assured smirk that drove Nettle crazy. He couldn't stand the sound of her voice, the way she watched him.

The restraints were removed when his attorney requested it, but two uniformed officers stayed in the room. The charges were reviewed. Nettle rubbed his wrists and squirmed. The officers exchanged glances behind Nettle's back. They had worked with Frost before. The questioning began.

Nettle started to react. When his attorney nudged Shade under the table, Nettle gave him a hard shove and turned on the prosecutor. "Look, I didn't mean to break that fool FBI guy's jaw! How was I supposed to know he was a law officer? Didn't get a good look at the silly badge he flashed. He grabbed my arm. Hear what I'm saying? Don't blow me off!" He looked like he wanted to punch Ms. Frost.

"May I have some time alone with my client?"

"Five minutes," Deputy Prosecutor Frost said. "Come on guys."

Nettle began ranting as the door closed. "Why do I have to put up with all this crap? Who does this bottled blond slut think she is, anyway? The bitch has blood-sucking eyes. Why does she drum those red talons? What's with this pink room? And the restraints?"

"You'd better turn into an ice man, Mr. Nettle. Do you realize you just confessed to battery on a FBI agent, after he showed you his badge? The jury's going to hear that in your own words, yelled right into the tape recorder."

"Hey, I had a plane to catch. He stopped me."

"Look, we've been over this. If you're going to plead guilty, let me see what kind of a deal we can work out. It's going to be better than a straight confession in here."

"I'm not confessing a thing to some bimbo."

"That prosecutor has locked up more tough guys than most folks in the office. If she can keep you steamed up, she'll nail you, sure as hell. Now get a grip!"

"I'm just a piece of meat, trapped prey. Luck, that was all. They got lucky. I won't say another word without getting your okay. I swear."

After the interrogation, in a private few minutes before he left, Nettle's attorney promised that he would be sure Nettle got a fair trial.

"But don't count on any deal for leniency. I'll explore it, but she's going to try to nail your ass. We could attack the credibility of the doorman, but he's a Vietnam vet with a Silver Star."

There were other problems the attorney didn't bring up.

He knew Nettle's wife, Angie, had filed for divorce, and Nettle could not prove he was anywhere else the night of the shooting at the Biltmore. But what the hell, it was a high profile case.

Since Kennedy International airport comes under federal jurisdiction, the U.S. Attorney's office looked at the case, but decided New York could have Shade Nettle. New York tried Shade Nettle for attempted murder and possession of an illegal, unregistered handgun, also a felony. He received eight to twenty-five years. In California, Canby International asked the state to file embezzlement charges against Nettle, along with the conspiracy to commit kidnapping count, so the statute of limitations would not run out while Nettle was New York's guest. The US Immigration Service also filed a deportation order, for the future, if and when Nettle finished his sentences. The matter of Jake Hartig was simpler.

At the trial in Sacramento, due to his lawyers' successful change in venue motion, Jake Hartig surprised everyone by replacing his legal team. The judge ordered a complete psychological evaluation. All the doctors, even those hired by the defense, determined that Jake Hartig was competent to stand trial. The judge had to remind himself that the competency threshold was low. The Sacramento jury found Jake Hartig guilty of assault with a deadly weapon on the Oakland city employee, soliciting a kidnapping, and conspiracy to commit fraud. The jury found him not guilty of embezzlement and not guilty of stealing city property, because he returned the van. He also received eight to twenty-five years.

\* \* \*

Carol knew the couple in the foyer of the Danville Hotel waiting to be seated when she and Diane arrived to have lunch.

"Well, it's the delta hero, our future Congresswoman." Carl Gard's voice could be heard by all but the totally deaf. He laughed, delighting in the scene he caused, knowing his antics didn't phase Carol.

Carol introduced Diane to Bea, who was trying good-naturedly to get her husband to quiet down, and to Carl.

"The announcer," Diane said. "I have a friend exactly like you across the bay, a dear friend.

When Carl learned that Diane had been the other woman with Carol in the delta, he felt further inspiration. "Both heroes from the delta."

"Heroines," his wife corrected.

"I like heroes. I consider it gender-neutral." Diane smiled at Carl as his wife tried to pull him away to his table.

He called back, "By the way, Carol, did you get our campaign donation? We had to take out a loan for it, so you have to win."

"I certainly did. A thousand dollars was most generous, even among friends."

"A thousand dollars? I thought you said we gave a hundred, dear." Carl turned dramatically to his wife.

Bea rolled her eyes. "You know perfectly well that we gave a thousand, Carl. Now pipe down or I'll write another check to her. I can, you know, in my name this time."

Carl chortled and finally sat down. "Had to let people know what the ante was, Dear." He watched Carol shake hands with several people and noticed that she selected the chair affording the best view of the dining room, although not of the entry.


"We mustn't let so much time pass without catching up with each other," Diane said. "What a wonderful foil your Carl is."

Carol raised one perfectly groomed eyebrow, and changed the subject. "Let me see your new ring."

"And let me see yours."

Carol's new wedding ring was a wide yellow band with a brilliant cut, full carat diamond. It was bold and lovely. Diane had replaced hers with a set as close to the original as possible.

"As beautiful as they are, they aren't as important now are they?"

"Oh, I don't know." Carol grinned. "This diamond is much bigger than the one I had before."

Diane laughed. "It's so important to take time for good friends, even if one of them is running for Congress." She caught the little sigh Carol made and realized that although Carol had said she needed the break, lunch could not take more than an hour. Neither one picked up the menu, too much catching up to do. The waiter brought iced tea at once. Diane watched Carol turn around to check the entrance and take another glance around the room before focusing on her visit. "You look much better than the last time we spent some time together. No traces of the bruises," Carol said.

"Well, the bruises are gone, yes. It's been almost two years. I'll always have this fishhook scar, though." Diane held up her hand and glanced at the marks between her thumb and forefinger.

"What about Roger? Last time we talked, he still was having some pain and stiffness where that bullet went through his collarbone".

"He's fine, except for his serve. It's not the smooth motion he had before he was shot. He's had to adjust it, and he doesn't get the same power he used to, which upsets him. Of course, we have less and less time for tennis these days."

"How's the foot?"

"It's fine too, after that last minor surgery to get it really cleaned out. You know I had to wear a klutzy booty around for six weeks while everything healed."

"You told me about it. Tough on such a busy person. And, speaking of being busy, I appreciate the chance to have lunch with you during a congressional campaign, Carol. I know it's a special favor."

"For old time's sake," Carol raised her glass in a toast.

"Yes."

"I thank you for sending your party's campaign strategy book when I first announced. And, especially for the candid notes you made on the various political consultants, Diane."

"Well, you have my thoughts, from my limited perspective. There definitely is a wide variation in ethical standards among the consultants too. You saw my notes. You'll get some idea of what you may be up against. Nothing is super secret. It's pretty general and most of it's common sense, but I thought it might help to have a feel for the opposition's consultant. Do you know who they're using?"

"Several different people so far. I think their campaign is trying out different ones for different assignments to get a feel for the personalities involved. Anyway, thank you very much. I have the binder in the car to return to you. Can't have it lying around the other party's campaign headquarters."

"Nor your house, I dare say." Diane laughed, fully aware that Carol never would have taken the binder to her campaign headquarters.

"You know the pretrial publicity has been a mixed blessing in this campaign. I mean it has taken time and energy, but it certainly has kept my name in the papers."

"Yes, I understand the importance of name recognition. Nobody opposed me for reelection last time. I see you've become a victims' rights champion, along with your environmental work and the Clean the Delta Campaign. When you advocated slowing the contracted water allotments to southern California, you must have been in every paper in the state."

As they chatted, Diane noticed a large man talking to the hostess who looked and pointed in their direction.

"Someone has just asked for you and is headed our way. Big man with thin brown hair, glasses and a slight limp." Diane spoke without a further glance in the man's direction.

"Sounds like Smolders, my chief opponent's big backer in the primary race."

Neither one had changed her carefree expression when Smolders arrived at their table. "Carol, the very person I have been looking for." His voice strained with forced warmth.

"Hello, Jack. I would like you to meet my good friend, Diane Lind. She's a political strategist from the Peninsula." Diane smiled at her new title, but she knew the Jack Smolders name from an earlier conversation with Carol.

Smolders took Diane's hand perfunctorily and returned his attention immediately to Carol, going so far as to turn one shoulder away from Diane. "I have a little gift for you, Carol. We've been on opposite sides recently, but I want you to know there are no hard feelings. It was a good fight, and you won it."

His voice still had a tinge of regret in it or Diane might have stayed silent. "The judge's DUI arrest helped." Diane spoke with a caustic smile, referring to Carol's opponent in the primary.

Smolders cleared his throat and put a small, thick manila envelope on the table. "Here's thirty-four thousand for your campaign. Call it a peace offering after that interview we put you through when we endorsed the judge. Some of us were for you all along, I assure you. There'll be more money. Not everyone's in town this summer. We also plan to donate much more through the party."

Diane saw Carol's wide eyes staring at Smolders, her hand touching the envelope, a finger tracing a corner of its outline on the tablecloth. Diane's thoughts were murderous. He must be very pleased with himself. He knows it's important. That she needs the money badly. She's only raised a hundred and eighty-three thousand. More will come, though, with her primary opponent out of the way. Public place like this. Everyone will know she has gone over to them by this afternoon. What was it he had said about her speeches? Environmental crap and campaign reform hogwash. Called her a friend of mindless code enforcement bureaucrats and old lady tree huggers. God knows what he says behind her back.

Carol's expression moved from surprise to control. She shot Diane a quick look. Diane answered with an almost

imperceptible shake of her head, cold blue eyes shouting "no."
The room had become silent. Carol drew a long, deep breath.
She put on her professional politician smile, not the warm, real
one she usually used on the campaign trail.

"Jack, I can't accept this, but, I've told you and all the others,
I remain open to hearing your concerns. I'll be happy to meet
with you and the Jefferson Trust group, to talk, anytime."

Carol's eyes tracked the envelope disappearing back into the
breast pocket of Smolder's silk suit. The room tentatively came
alive again. Few people had heard Carol's reply but the message
of the returned envelope shouted clearly. Smolders straightened
stiffly, drew a long slow breath, stared at the small vase of
miniature pink roses and baby's breath on the table with glazed
eyes.

"Thank you for your time, Carol. I'll be in touch."

Furtive glances followed his muttering progress from the
room. "Damn female politicians."

"Way to go, Carol," Carl Gard boomed across the room and
added a thumbs up sign. The smile Carol returned was a little
weak. She moved four fingers in a tiny wave.

"You'll get some of the money, anyway." Diane said. "They
can't afford not to back you, however reluctantly, and now it will
be on your terms."

"I don't know. What's to stop them from backing my
opponent, the one from your party? Other than he is suing
Smolders in a property dispute," she answered her own question
with a look of malicious pleasure. She pulled out her daily
planner and squeezed in a notation between the one thirty and
two p.m. space that had been part of her time reserved for lunch.

"I need to call the person in charge of my fund-raising
efforts. Her group has been very successful so far. We have a
number of corporate sponsors and business people coming out
who haven't been involved in the past. 'Course, I know part of
that is due to Roger's position at Canby International, but I also
get good responses to my message. I'd be lying if I said we were
near our goal, though. It takes so darn much. I need to ask my

fund raising committee to cast a wider net than we discussed for the August reception. The corporate grounds where we're having it and the three other corporate sponsors are prominently displayed on the invitation. Along with the environmental groups, trade unions, several of the law-enforcement associations.

"The invitations go to the printer tomorrow. I was thinking we should see if Smolders' crowd wants to be added to the list, but the committee has probably thought of it. Maybe we should call them again, before press time."

"Nothing like a candidate's mind at work," said Diane.

Reaching for her iced tea, Carol turned and checked the entrance again. "Oops! What a mess." The brown liquid flooded across the crisp, pure white tablecloth and sank into it. She tried to blot it with her napkin. A waiter hurried to do the same, while the brown stain tinged anything touching it.

Diane pulled her chair back to the table, moving her eyes from the tablecloth to Carol's face, back to the table and then to the window.

"Oh, Diane, I have great news. You met Hsing Tom, the VP of Finance. Well, when I win, his daughter has agreed to work in my local office. She receives her Master's degree in political science next month, and she's eager to add some practical knowledge to her theoretical base."

"That's great. By the way, any member of the news media here now?"

"No, no one I know, at least." Carol glanced around the room again. "Wait, the publisher of our local paper — his wife is here, over by the window near the Gards, woman in the green silk dress."

Diane grinned deliciously. "Even if no story appears about this little incident, your credibility with the media is inviolate."

"I wish you would change your mind about coming to Washington with me. My offer is still good. You're always thinking."

"You think having a registered Republican on your staff will make you look broad-minded. I do ask that you hear me out on controversial educational issues. I don't believe you'll violate any democratic principles, with either a big 'D' or small 'd,' by doing that, besides I'm very liberal on the issue of the nation's children. Nothing's more important."

"Actually, you're pretty liberal on everything." Carol smiled. Diane smiled back. "It shows that one shouldn't place too much importance on party labels, doesn't it? I don't care much for liberal or conservative either. People use them to judge whether or not to listen or talk with others, whether to let them in or freeze them out.

"I would suggest that you take California Elected Women back to Washington with you, though. Here in the rarified political climate of the Bay Area, we are accustomed to thinking in terms of political equality and you and I, especially, have been so involved working with elected women. You'll be a distinct minority in Washington. There'll be some ugly times, but you know that."

"I'll remember the CEW concepts. If things get too rough, we'll organize. Evelyn Day was talking about a Washington reception for the women of California's delegation, actually for all of California's delegation, but sponsored by CEW."

"So, what do you hear about the trial? Does your attorney have anything new?" asked Diane. The facts still shocked them, and talking helped.

"I'll never get over the treachery of Shade Nettle," said Carol. "What an evil person. And that slimy Jake Hartig — apparently, he was blackmailing Shade for a percentage."

"I understand there is a possible drug charge too. Methamphetamine," said Diane. "At least, Jake was a user."

"Seems that way. Roger didn't even know about Jake, but he thought Nettle probably was working with someone. Jake had been given his notice. Shade and Jake wanted to have Roger murdered, and they would have had us killed! You saw the FBI report. That Rudy character is believed to have killed at least three people."

"Did you hear that Hartig wanted to turn state's evidence and testify against Nettle when he learned how much evidence the police have?" Diane asked.

"Well, Nettle's being tried in New York," Carol said. "And New York has all they need. California has Hartig six ways to Sunday with his notes on the kidnappers, the pictures at the houseboat and the police sergeant's identification of him as the man who bailed Jimmy Thrasher out of jail after Roger was mugged."

"And, his fingerprints turned up in the stolen East Bay Municipal District's truck," Diane said. She noticed Carol looked around frequently as they talked. There was a pause. Carol turned back to Diane.

"The driver identified Hartig as the man who hit him and left him in the back, tied up and bleeding," Carol said.

"I still haven't figured out what on earth Hartig wanted with the East Bay MUD truck." Diane ran a finger across her lower lip in thought. "Is he still in the hospital?"

"He was in some psychiatric ward in Oakland, last time I heard. Was it at Highland? Anyhow, while he was out on bail, he was picked up second time on a fifty-one fifty. I still can't believe he was granted bail. That will probably be his defense, insanity."

"Yeah," said Diane. "I know about those seventy-two hour holds for psychiatric evaluation. After his last release, he committed himself a week later, according to my attorney. I wonder if he's still there. Is Vacaville where they put the criminally insane?"

Carol sipped her ice water. "I guess so. I knew something was wrong when that man took our pictures while we were walking into the stockholders' meeting. I'm so glad that Al Gonzales had nothing to do with any of this. He's such a sweet guy. The police and FBI really upset him when they hauled him in for questioning. His name and address were in Hartig's files somewhere."

The women had given their sworn statements and had been prepared by their attorneys.

"Where do you suppose our old rings are now?" asked Carol without looking up from the menu.

"In a pawn shop or, more likely, somewhere in an area scattered around that old houseboat, where the ski boat blew up." Diane studied the menu.

"Just think, they could be deep in that black mud at the bottom of the slough," Carol said. "Ugh."

"Or, in some fish's stomach. They might have been great lures."

"I can't stand it, Diane. I was going to have the fish until we started talking about the delta. How did we get onto that?" She changed the subject. "I received a campaign contribution from Louise Renne, the City Attorney of San Francisco. She's such a nice la—."

"Don't say that."

"She's great." Carol retrenched. She knew better.

"Yes, she's doing an outstanding job as CEW's president this year too." Diane said. "She must never sleep. Did you know that she alerted the Highway Patrol when we didn't show up in Sacramento?"

"Yeah, I did," Carol said. "Her motives aren't completely pure for the contribution, however. I had to promise to be one of the keynote speakers at the March conference."

Their lunches arrived, scarcely interrupting their conversation.

Carol watched the other customers whenever new people were seated. She waved and greeted those she knew, and made mental notes to go by their tables before she left. During a rare lull in their chatting, Carol's expression became serious, and she concentrated her gaze directly on her friend's eyes.

"You knew that boat would blow up, didn't you?"

177

Nothing changed in Diane's expression, not the smiling lips, not the tilt of her head, no flight of an eyebrow. Only the deep, warm blue of her irises intensified to a frosty, hard, ice, then liquid vulnerability, pain, and flickered back to warmth again. Carol saw the changes.

Diane asked, "Did you know that my father was a naval officer?" Carol didn't answer. Diane glanced away. "It was an old boat. One must take all the safety precautions." Then she looked directly at Carol and said, "An innocent person could have been killed in that boat."

"Not likely, Carol said. "Not at all likely. It would have been either the kidnappers or the ones who ordered and conspired in the kidnapping, Nettle or Hartig, someone who had a key."

"An acceptable risk of war?"

"I've never thought of it in those terms before, but I'm learning. Politics can be very much like combat. I'm glad you're on my side."

"I've wondered if I was the one in the bunker or the one on the beach. Fifty years after the war and that bunker claimed another casualty. I was the one —."

"Shut up, Diane. You're not making sense. Don't say such things."

Diane heeded the warning and reached down to the floor. "I brought you a little gift in honor of today and what we went through together."

"I've been wondering about that package."

Diane handed her the box wrapped in cheery paper and tied with a kelly green ribbon. Taking the package, Carol found it to be extremely light. She turned it in one hand, then shook it. She gave Diane a quizzical expression. She unwrapped it carefully, opened the lid and slowly withdrew a rectangular, wicker-like object. "It's a —. Oh, let me guess. It must be a cricket cage."

"For luck. That's only if you catch your own cricket."

"I shall treasure it, Diane, undoubtedly without the cricket. It's perfect."

Two weeks later, Diane received a call from Carol. "I'm faxing you a draft of my position paper on education. I've been working on it with a couple of advisors, and I'm satisfied it strikes a good balance. You'll like it. Most of it. All of it. You know how these things have to sound."

"Have to sound? Most of it?"

"Just certain words, phrases that will resonate with the voters."

"Not vouchers, I hope."

"No, but I've been asked about them. I'm not ruling them out. You understand. We have been very careful with the wording."

"I'm getting confused about who's the Democrat and who's the Republican in this conversation."

"Cut it out. You can't simply throw more money at these problems."

"Carol — "

"What?"

"You took Smolders' money."

Silence.

"I — . You don't understand. There'll be construction jobs."

"Ah, Carol, I do." Diane filled her lungs with air, calming the revulsion building in her stomach.

"Diane, I need you. I need an honest friend, a good friend."

"In that case, I must tell you to drop that ridiculous cliche about throwing more money at education. California is determined to dig itself into dead last in per pupil spending among the fifty states. And you know it.

"I wish you well. When you want my opinion on issues, I'll give it to you, but I'm guessing this is the last time."

Carol replaced the receiver. "You're right. I don't need you at all."

# Chapter 19

## Rayburn House Office Building, Washington D.C., January 1995

Congresswoman Carol Steadhold, a Democrat in the Republican tide washing over the city, threaded her way into her musty, isolated office through the boxes of supplies that her staff was busily unpacking and sometimes repacking and pushing in corners. Along with her briefcase, which contained her draft proposal for a tougher clean water bill, she arrived carrying a package in a small plastic grocery bag to protect it from the blowing flurries outside.

Sally Hampshire, the appointments secretary, ticking off the day's schedule, followed her into the private office. The California congresswoman disentangled herself from her layers of damp wool clothes and carefully unwrapped the package with only an occasional nod. The appointments secretary stopped talking and watched her boss.

"This, Sally, is a cricket cage. It's for good luck."

Carol surveyed her cramped office for an appropriate place for her good luck charm. Sally caught sight of the glossy dark insect with long, graceful antennae inside. "And he is the cricket?"

Carol was ready for any "feeding crickets is not in my job description" comments, but Sally kept quiet.

"She"

"What?"

"*She*, not he. I painstakingly saved her from a boring entomology journal in the Library of Congress." Noticing her scheduler's look of shocked disapproval, she added, "It's not what you think. Members of Congress have access to a color copier. With an exacto knife and a little double-sided tape, I have my cricket. Her name is Diane, for Diane Lind. She's on the list of contributors.

"Type out a little thanks for the cricket cage for me to sign, please. Tell her about the paper cricket named Diane to remind me of her."

Four months later, Sally moved from where she was standing at aide Jenny Walker's desk and darted into Carol Steadhold's office right behind the congresswoman. Bob Jackson, also in a rush, was right behind the scheduler. Sally knew the congresswoman had only five minutes if she were going to be on time for the dinner in Alexandria. Bob could try to have his say in the hall as Carol Steadhold was leaving.

Carol must have felt hounded. "Doesn't anyone want to know how the hearing went?"

"No time," said Sally, who had a very small sense of humor. "Foregone conclusion. Straight party line vote. Right?"

Carol Steadhold rubbed the back of her neck and looked at the worn carpet, then the ceiling. Sally used her self-important voice. "Tomorrow, Pacific Rim trade policy working breakfast at eight, downstairs. It's on your calendar. The hearings on the Clean Water bill at one. Better leave the mayors' box lunch meeting here at twelve thirty to be sure you get to the hearing on time. You're the second person to testify. Blue folder there on your desk. I highlighted the main points. Cover the highlights. Drop the back up unless you're asked. Make them use their time, not yours."

"Thank you, Sally." Carol opened her folder, glanced at the neat pages and put the folder in her briefcase.

"Congresswoman, I -" Bob Jackson stopped when Carol raised her hand, and Sally jumped in again, but Carol interrupted. "Three mayors from my district helped write the bill I introduced that was killed last week. Tell the mayors I have to testify. Invite them to the hearing, Sally, if you can reach them. Let them see firsthand what I'm facing."

"I must interrupt!" Bob turned to face Sally with both of his hands in the air, and then he turned to face the congresswoman.

"I can tell you, in confidence, that the committee is going to change their hearing schedule to seven forty-five a.m. It's a ploy to eliminate your testimony all together. Your's, Congresswoman Eshoo's and the people from the Department of Interior the administration is sending over."

"We'll ask them to reschedule."

"No dice. They plan to shut the hearings down, completely down, by noon. The chairman will decide who testifies and for how long, and the people opposing our position are part of the mix."

Carol Steadhold set her jaw and resisted asking her aide if he was absolutely sure of his information. Instead she shifted back to Sally. "Call around. Find out where the mayors' association is holding their conference. See if you can reach Jan Edwards or Bob Riley and see if they can get our group to the hearing room at seven thirty because the hearing has been called for ..." She paused for Bob.

"Seven forty-five."

"We should alert Anna's office too," said Carol.

"I sent an anonymous e-mail to Rider at Interior and to Eshoo's office," said Bob, "but they'll probably think it's a dirty trick."

"Send another, under my name this time. Sally, give me a copy of the schedule for the rest of tomorrow, I've got to run."

At five forty-five that afternoon, Sally briefed the congresswoman on the updated schedule, gestured with her pencil, and accidentally knocked the cricket cage to the floor. As she replaced it on the bookshelf, she blew the dust from it. "I need to get in here with a dust cloth. Diane, right?"

"What?" Carol glanced at Sally, saw the small cage. "Oh. Diane. Yes."

"A friend from California, I gather?"

"Umm, Diane Lind."

"Should I put her on the VIP list?'

"Nah, treat her like any other constituent. She doesn't even live in my district."

"Ouch."

"Okay, put her on the list, but she's not that important, politically."

"You should stay in touch with friends. People around here carry knives. Call her tonight."

"You're over-stepping, Sally."

"Eighteen years on the Hill speaking to you, Congresswoman." Sally said, "With respect," and was out the door.

There had been notes, Carol reflected. There was her personal thank you for the campaign contribution, written on the back of the form letter. After the election, Diane wrote a congratulatory card with a few sentences and exclamation points. That was it. Congresswoman Carol Steadhold didn't have much time to care, and Diane Lind probably understood.

Carol pulled up her e-mail address book and found Diane Lind but only a telephone number. She looked at her crystal desk clock. Close to nine on the West Coast. She dialed.

After the pleasantries and her "just to talk" explanation, Carol said, "I've learned the political consensus dance, Diane. One has a good idea and does the homework, then calls Two. Two doesn't like being pushed, but recognizes the idea as good, so calls Three with the idea and claims credit. Knowing this might happen, One had initialed the idea. Two could remove the initials, but usually doesn't bother, claims credit anyway. Three likes the idea, irrespective of its origin, and implements it for the good of the cause. Or, Three hates the idea and buries it, with the appropriate flowers and phrases. Extra steps, twists and turns may be added to make a true fandango."

"You're rambling, Carol. Sounds like you have the process down pat."

"I should. I've played all the parts."

"Really?"

Anyone in this place who claims she hasn't is lying, or a complete incompetent."

"Why the confession?"

"Lack of sleep, PMS, who knows?"

"PMS?"

"Oh, shut up." Carol shorted then drew a long breath. "It was you, Diane. You were the first."

"The first what?"

"You gave me the first lessons in the political dance, the basic steps."

"Does that make me friend or foe? You were a mayor when we met. You knew plenty."

"You'll always be a friend, Diane. It's just that some times I need to be reminded."

Congresswoman Carol Steadhold need not have kept them, the caged paper cricket and the outspoken secretary, but she did.

# Epilogue

In 1996, Brad Lind retired, and his wife, Diane, finished her third four-year term and retired also. They remodeled their house to enlarge their home office.

Due to her service to the schools, Diane had a collection of commemorative apples, a couple of engraved, old-fashioned, school bells, and numerous plaques and certificates of appreciation and commendation. She rejected the idea of a vanity wall. She had other things to pursue. Diane repacked the plaques and framed certificates, all but one. It was not the most meaningful, but it was large and had a nice frame, with colorful blue matting and the golden Seal of the State of California. In the tiny bathroom that once had been two large closets, she hung it over the toilet and smiled.

# About The Author

Linda Lanterman, one of the Sierra Writers, lives in Auburn, California and Kailua-Kona, Hawaii. She earned her Bachelor's Degree in Political Science from the University of California, Berkeley. She taught freshman political science at the University of Georgia, Athens, while she earned her Master's Degree in American Government and International Relations.

Her rich sense of character and setting developed early. "My parents taught us to see everything, to notice how prejudice and power mingle in our daily lives. They also taught my brothers and me to examine our presumptions. We had lively family discussions of politics, literature and philosophy. My parents inspired me to strive to be a force for good."

Lanterman held both elected and appointed positions in California. She remains interested in education and public policy. "I need to understand the forces at work behind the scenes, all the elements that go into decision-making. Where is the real power in a group or in the community? Who exercises it? How? What motives drive each individual's actions? How can I best use this knowledge to help all young people and the whole community?"

Printed in the United States
965700002B